The Heavenly Life

A Remarkable Book

SOME WOMEN I HAVE KNOWN

❀ ❀ BY *❀ ❀*

REV. J. B. CULPEPPER.

CLOTH, 75c.   *❀❀*   PAPER, 40c.

Here is a most remarkable book. It grips the reader from the first page and holds him to the last. Chapters on "Mother," "Catharine," "My First Circuit Mother," "A Bottle of Tears," etc., etc., are just simply wonderful. The book is worthy of an immense circulation.

SOME WORDS OF COMMENDATION

A leading Presbyterian minister in Kentucky said before a large audience, "I heartily wish I could give away 1,000 copies of that book. I know it will bless every home it enters."

A Presbyterian minister in Mississippi said: "That chapter on 'mother' will make me love Bro Culpepper forever."

When seated at the dinner table another preacher's wife said: "Why, husband, what is the matter with your eyes?" "Wife, I have been reading Bro. Culpepper's book, 'Some Women,' and have been laughing and 'boo-hooing' for two hours."

A Georgia mother wrote: "Send me another copy of 'Some Women,' there are half a dozen fussing over this one, and I can't get to it at all."

A young woman from Wisconsin writes: "Our large family have all read your new book, Bro. Culpepper's 'Some Women.' We have read it more than once around and have enjoyed it very much. We all thank you for writing it."

STIRS EVERY READER THROUGH AND THROUGH.

A THRILLING, SOUL - MOVING, SOUL - WINNING BOOK.

IT BRINGS THE HEART INTO THE THROAT AND TEARS TO THE EYES.

PUBLISHER'S PREFACE.

In each generation God raises some few saints who discern truth more deeply than their fellows; rare spirits to whom He opens truths long hidden from the world, and such as are specially needed for the generation. These are marvelous times. Not only is the material world all agog, but the spiritual is also astir. The commercial spirit is materializing the race, and the churches frequently have more of form, ceremony, wealth, social position and prestige than of religious fervor, spiritual discernment and holy aggressiveness. The age is evil (Gal. 1:4), but the coming of Jesus in kingly glory is nearing, and God is raising up men of far-seeing capacity who are unfolding the deep truths of revelation as the needed lessons for the age. Lovers of the Word divine will surely welcome these pages. They are full of deep, soul-nourishing truth, that will prove a great incentive to prayer, meditation and holy aggressiveness. We bespeak for the chapters that follow an attentive reading by all who love our Lord Jesus in sincerity.

CONTENTS.

CHAPTER I.

"Like the days of heaven upon earth." This is the promise the Lord gave to Israel when they went into Canaan, if they would obey Him (Deut. 11:21). The heavenly life, and the heavenly kingdom are all alike; they are not of, or out from, this world, but they are to come down from God, out of the heavens, and exist on this earth. All true life on this earth went into bankruptcy with the fall of Adam. Since then, all true life is from above, and founded in redemption. There is a passage in Col. 3:1-4 which contains a wonderful setting forth of the heavenly life. Three great facts are stated regarding the heavenly life, namely: It is a supernatural life, a hidden life, and then a life to be revealed.

1. *It is a Supernatural Life.* "If ye then be risen with Christ, seek those things which are above, where Christ sitteth on the right hand of God. Set your affection (or, more literally, your imagination) on things above."

Here we have the great secret of the heavenly life, in that it is a life in union with Christ, a life that flows into us from having our spirits grafted into Christ by the Holy Ghost, a life which incessantly flows down into us, like the blood from the heart coursing down to the

(5)

lower extremity of the body, so from the infinite Christ, who, during this dispensation, is seated at the right hand of God, His heavenly life comes streaming down to us. There are two words which we need clearly to understand at the outset in this exposition. The first word is "risen." We inquire what is meant by being "risen with Christ." It is not the same word as that used for the resurrection. The Greek word for resurrection is *"anastasio,"* from *"ana"* (again), and *"stasis"* (to stand up), and is used especially to mean the resurrection, or the standing up again of the dead body that was laid down in the grave. A great many people, not having accurate knowledge of Scripture, speak of the soul's conversion as being a resurrection, and some call it "the first resurrection." This is a mistake, as the first resurrection spoken of in Scripture is applied only to saints, and instead of the new birth being the first resurrection, it is distinctly revealed that we must be justified, regenerated and sanctified in order to have a place in the first resurrection. "Blessed and holy is he that hath part in the first resurrection." (Rev. 20:6.) When we are awakened and born of the Spirit, our human spirits, which have been dead in sin, do rise up from moral death, but it is not a rising again like the standing up of a dead body that had previously stood upright in living vigor; hence this word, "to be risen with Christ," does not in any sense take the place of the resurrection of our bodies, nor does it imply that fanatical notion that we are now glorified, and will never die. It is the moral, the spiritual being, that has risen from a state of nature and sin into a state of grace by a living faith in the ascended Savior. Another word we need to understand, is the expression, "Where Christ sitteth at the right hand of God." So many people speak of Christ as at present sitting on His own throne, which is entirely unscriptural. Every passage in the Bible describing the present location of the glorified body of Jesus speaks of Him as being "on the Father's throne," "at the right hand of the throne of God," "at the right hand of the majesty on high," and the Father saying to Him during this present age, "Sit thou at my right hand, until I make thy enemies thy footstool." Thus every Scripture speaks of Christ in this age as at the right hand of the Father, on the Father's throne. But on the other hand, every single Scripture that speaks of Christ sitting on His own throne, uniformly fixes the time of His occupancy of His throne at His second coming. So, be careful never to confound the sitting of Jesus at the right hand of the Father in the present age, with the sitting of Christ on His own Messianic throne in the age to come. With this explanation of these two words, let us notice more particularly the heavenly life the true believer has in this dispensation, by virtue of being in heart, and by a living faith, united to Christ. All life is a fathomless mystery. The life in a grain of corn, or an egg, or the root of a tree, is hidden from all our five senses, from all science, from all comprehension, and as deeply shrouded in God's omnipotence as the life of any plant, or animal, or angel in the most distant world or space. God only knows what life is. He alone can originate life, and establish the laws by which every kind of life can reproduce itself. When we

are regenerated, the life of Christ is imparted to our
human spirits, through the organ of the human heart
and by the agency of the Holy Ghost. We are told in
Scripture that the Father gave His Son power to have
life in Himself, and that the Son gives His life to those
who truly believe in Him. This imparted divine life is
more than thought; it is more than action, for it leads
to action; it is more than all good works, for it is the
seed from which all the good works sprout, just as the
life of a tree is more than the leaves and the fruit which
it produces. The essence of this heavenly life is Divine
love communicated to our spiritual organism. Just as
trees and animals and men are living organisms, so the
soul is a living organism, into which the life of Christ
is injected through the living word of promise. This
heavenly life has instinctive affinities for the supernatural. It has modes of nourishment, and laws of
growth, and possibilities of celestial flower and fruitage,
similar to other species of life. In a certain sense, men
may live many kinds of lives. Some live a political, others a scientific life; yet others live a financial life, by
which the ruling passion subsidizes to itself all the energies and capabilities of the man. Just so, it is possible
to live a love life, even in the human as well as the divine. For instance, here is an excellent woman who is
in love with, and espoused to, a true gentleman. It is
expedient, in order to gain an immense fortune, that he
leave his native land, also the object of his love, and
cross the seas to some distant country, there to spend a
few years in patiently looking after his estate. When
he goes away, the heart, the thought, the imagination—

in one sense, the very life of the woman that loves him, goes along with him to that distant land, and she more truly lives in his life and with him in that distant land, than with the people and in the locality where her body sojourns. This is the exquisite picture that is set forth in this passage of Scripture. If we are thoroughly espoused to Christ and have His life in our hearts, then with His ascension to the right hand of God the Father, there goes up with Him the secret fountains of all our inner being; and our hearts, our thoughts, rise with Him; our imaginations and longings, our hopes and dreams fly toward Him, ever hovering around Him; and we paint ideal pictures of Him and His glorious surroundings in that radiant land whither He has gone to gather the materials of His coming kingdom. The word "affection" in this passage is in the margin "mind." There are four Greek words translated mind—one signifies the apprehending faculty, another the reasoning faculty, another the judging or determining faculty, and yet another signifies the imaginative faculty, the power of fancy, the artistic or picture-making power of the mind. The word we are now speaking of, and which is translated "affection," is, in the Greek, "*phronos,*" from which we make the word "phrenology," and signifies the imaginative part of the mind. Hence we are to seek after those things which pertain to Christ, and set our fond imagination to building thought-pictures of Jesus and Paradise and the saints and the angels and the coming of the Lord and the coronation day, of the rich and manifold rewards, of the glorious kingdom, and the city of pure gold, and of the long, bright ages that stretch away in a successive series of ever-increasing splendor, world without end. If the mind must build air-castles, let us build them in the heavens. The true believer in this present life is like a diver in the sea. As a man puts on a diving bell and descends to the bottom of the ocean and is supplied with fresh air by an air pump on the ship over his head, so the believer is to put on the baptism of the Holy Ghost from heaven and live down in this lower world surrounded and pressed on every side by the dark waters of this present evil age, and draw down from the right hand of God the vital breath of heaven through the mediation of Jesus. The diver can live down in the sea, provided he has fresh air from the top, and provided the sea does not get into him. In like manner we can live the heavenly life down in this world, if we only get our prayer breath from Christ, and providing the world is kept out of us.

2. *It is a hidden life.* "For ye are dead, and your life is hid with Christ in God." The word "dead" here does not of course refer to the physical death, but to being crucified in heart with Christ, being dead to sin and to this present world. Conversion is a birth, and sanctification is a death. How strange that so many cannot see the difference between these two spiritual conditions. By the grace of sanctification we utterly die to this present world, its life, spirit, aims, honors, notions and desires, and we are thereby put out of joint with all its affairs and adjusted to another kingdom which is to come. When anything dies, its life passes out beyond the range of observation, and no one can follow it by any manifestation which it gives forth.

This is exactly the double thought stated here by the apostle. As long as a man is living his natural life, the world can recognize it, but when some day the stroke of the sword of God's Word slays that man's natural life and he dies to sin and all the world, he is, like a dead man, an offensive corpse in the eyes of the world, and his life has slipped away into such inscrutable secrecy as to be beyond the knowledge and all comprehension of his fellows. As I have said before, every form of life is a secret, hidden in fathomless depths beyond all human knowledge. If no microscope and no science can find the life in a grain of wheat or a hen's egg, how much less is that divine life imparted to the soul by the Holy Ghost within the range of all human recognition as to what it is, and how it subsists, and what are its everlasting results. As God only knows the love of God, so God alone knows the secrets of His own life.

You will notice there is a double hiding of the heavenly life referred to in this passage. Our life is hid with Christ, and then Christ, in this present age, is hidden from the world up in the heavens with the Father. In our temperate zones, when winter comes on, vegetation dies, the vines and fruit trees shed their foliage, and to all appearance to the eyes of men, they are dead. The life in the tree or vine runs back into the root and hides itself there; and then the root is hidden in the ground. This is an exact likeness of the double hiding of the heavenly life in this present dispensation. Jesus is the vine, the root, and true believers are the branches. We are now living in the winter of faith. When we are crucified with Christ it is like the blight of a killing frost to the verdure and foliage of our natural, earthly lives, and we pass down into the baptism of death, and the world sees us no more, except in the language of David, "as dead men out of mind," and they cannot follow that swift retreat which our inner lives have made into Christ, the root of David, and the root of holy hearts and pure faith. And then they cannot see the Root, the immortal Jesus, for He is concealed beyond the blue sky, with the Father in the heavens.

There are several Scriptures in which the time of Christ's absence from the earth is compared to winter, and His return compared to the coming of summer. (See Song of Solomon, 2:10, 11; Matt. 24:32, 33.) It seems that very few Christians have enough discernment to heartily accept of this humiliating truth, that in order to be locked up in this hidden life of Christ, we must really die a death that will make us as uninteresting to men as trees stripped of all their gay foliage by the blasts of winter are dull and unattractive to the natural eye. So many people want a kind of religion that is attractive to the world, being ignorant of the fact that neither Jesus nor the apostles had that fascinating kind, but their very heavenly beauties were offensive to men, and they were hunted like wild beasts. The only religion that looks beautiful to the world is that which is invented by the devil. Christians who are so eager to make a good impression on men, always fail to make a good impression in heaven, and in spite of themselves the secret desire to have a religion that pleases men is an offensive displeasure to Almighty God. Jesus, to the world, is a leafless, bloomless "root out of a dry ground," and He never becomes "the Rose of Sharon," or "the Lily of the valley," except to anointed eyes—to those who are baptized into His death by the Holy Ghost and enter that hidden life, of which this present world knows nothing at all.

Those whose hearts are locked up with Jesus walk this earth in the present age as princes in disguise. They move around in the temporal duties of life like private detectives in a distant and unfriendly nation. They are breathing prayers, and thinking thoughts, and nursing hot fires of love, and ruminating on vast and amazing events that stretch over coming times and distant worlds. They are silently loading themselves up with a divine dynamite, that Daniel and Jesus both tell us will some day grind the kingdoms of this present world to powder. Their joys are hidden, for it is written "that a stranger doth not intermeddle with it." And their sorrows, also, are cloistered in the ear and bosom of God, for they know they need not look to the people of the world, and not even to the people of the church, for heart-felt sympathy; and so, like venturesome pioneers, they leave the crowded walks of life and traverse the great, solitary mountains, and take up claims on new and unexplored territory, and hold communion with the unseen God, and are more at home amid the great snowy mountain peaks of the divine perfection, than with the crowds that live only for the flesh and time.

The saints are called in Scripture "the hidden ones." Their life is doubly hidden, in the Son and in the Father. God says to them, "Call unto me, and I will show you great and hidden things." Their life is constantly fed by secret prayer. Their good deeds are to be folded in such quiet modesty, that the left hand (the goat) shall not know what the right hand (the sheep) doeth. The prophet says of the Almighty, "Verily, thou art a God that hidest thyself," and we are told on several occasions that "Jesus hid himself" from the crowd. God is working, as it were, by stealth, in this present age, and moves softly amid the affairs of life, as if shod with wool. The uncrucified life is not hidden, but showy, and makes great appearances, and seeks to be known, whether in church or in state. When we sink into God, like submarine ships down in the sea, we pass out of sight of the natural world and the natural man.

3. *The heavenly life is to be revealed.* "When Christ, our life, shall appear, then shall ye also appear with Him in glory." Please notice that the unfolding of all the secrets, and graces, and powers, and fruitage of the lives of the saints, is put right in connection with the return and visible appearing of the Son of man. All the Scriptures that bear on any one given thing always agree in their teaching on that subject. Hence, throughout all Scripture the second coming of Christ is referred to as the time when all hidden things shall "be manifested," "appear," "be revealed," and openly seen and known. It is at the time when Christ comes again, that "the thoughts of all hearts are to be revealed," when all secret prayers are to be "rewarded openly," when all faithfulness and unfaithfulness is to receive an open attestation, "when every hidden thing shall be brought to light," and when "the vail that now

covers all flesh shall be taken away," and when "the mystery shall be finished," and when "they shall see eye to eye in Zion," and when "we shall know even as we are known."

It will astonish you to take a concordance and hunt up the words "reveal" and "manifest," and kindred terms, and find how full the Bible is on what is to be made visible when Jesus returns and openly shows Himself to all the nations. That is when Paul expressly declares this heavenly life, which is now doubly hid, shall appear, with all things pertaining to it, in visible glory. God is forever working from the unseen to the visible, from darkness to light, from the secret to the known, from mystery to manifestation, from the inner to the outer. He first created the substance of the universe, and afterwards He said, "Let there be light." He first gave the shadow of good things to come, and then revealed the substance in Jesus. The Jehovah-Messiah was in this world, talking to prophets, giving laws, inspiring Scripture, receiving worship, and arranging providence, for four thousand years, and then was made flesh and became visible, and was seen and heard and touched by thousands, and visibly ascended to heaven till the time when His kingdom also shall become visible.

Human theology has coined a great many doctrines exactly opposite to the Bible, and because human nature is contrary to God, these unscriptural doctrines find ready acceptance by the majority of even professed Christians. One of these unscriptural doctrines concerning the future state is, that all things are going to be sublimated into a vague intellectualism and idealism, away from the solid and definite and sensible creation which God instituted at the beginning, and pronounced it very good. Swedenborgianism is simply old heathen Brahmanism remodeled and mixed with some Bible truth, and it accordingly contradicts the literal, historic facts of Scripture, and denies that there will be any literal resurrection of the dead body, or a visible return of the glorified humanity of Jesus. It is only one of the demon kind of last-day religions of the intellect and fancy, and, like what is falsely called *"Christian* Science" and Theosophy, teaches a lie under the pretense of presenting a religion so fine, so etherial, so intellectual, so exquisitely and sublimely spiritual, as never to be contaminated with anything so gross as the blood shed out of the real body of Jesus, or with a real resurrected human body, or with a literal heavens and new earth, be their skies ever so blue, or the mountains and plains ever so filled with vernal beauty, and singing birds and happy, God-loving, substantial generations of men. Thousands of elegant religious teachers in these latter days are getting too fine to believe in the plain, old-fashioned words of the God that made them. The most popular teaching in these heretical days, is that everything is traveling toward a lofty, intangible, invisible, inaudible sort of intellectualism—a kind of thin ghost-smoke of God's great creation.. Now, the fact is, that all creation, and all Scripture, and all history, is directly the opposite of such foolish teaching.

We are moving toward the age of open revelation, of glorious manifestation, when everything and every creature will be more distinctly recognized and more intensely individualized, than in the present age. Everything in creation travels from secrecy to open manifestation, and from indefinite thought and force toward well-rounded, well-defined life and action, to solidity of personality and character.

Creation was first formless, and in darkness; then came the moving of the Holy Ghost to produce solid forms and life; next came the outshining of light (Gen. 1:1-3). Every building on earth today, the palaces, the great monuments, the vast bridges, the swift-flying steamships, and palatial railway trains, at one time were only thoughts, vague ideas, little, dreamy inventions that teased some busy brain, till, step by step, the unseen ideas became visible, and shadowy imaginations sailed forth and anchored and developed themselves into forms of solid grandeur. The statues, the poems, the paintings, and the mighty music that charm millions today, were once silent feelings and fancies that fluttered noiselessly in some soul. The sinful thought of today becomes the open, solid crime of tomorrow. The unknown loving or heroic desire in the heart of a child comes forth in a few years in open manifestation of the matchless deeds of a Wesley or a Washington.

When we speak of the return of Jesus as being the time when His kingdom shall break forth into a sudden and visible glory over all the earth, and when the glorified "saints shall rule the nations with a rod of iron," in the exact language of Jesus, thousands of professing Christians, who only see one edge of prophetic truth, seem horrified, and begin to talk about Christ's kingdom not being of this world, and its being only a spiritual kingdom, and that it would degrade the dignity of Jesus and saints to live and reign on a visible and material world. In most cases these very people are swayed by love of money, love of church office, and church honor, and fine houses, and furniture, and politics, and society pride, loaded down with the earth and carnality, but pretending to have a religion that is too sublimated and etherial to walk on a redeemed planet, or touch the precious body of the glorified Jesus. Certainly Christ's "Kingdom is not of the world," or, as the Greek has it, "out from the world"; neither was Jesus of the world, but He lived and died on it without losing His holiness, or one trait of His matchless character; and according to Scripture He will live here again. The Bible is not *of* the world, but it is *in* the world, and being circulated by millions of copies. The saints, Jesus tells us, are not of the world, even as He Himself is not of the world, but they are in the world, and about fifty passages of Scripture inform us that in the coming age they will "inherit" and "possess" and "judge" and "rule" the world. The Son of God and the glorified saints can live on this green earth, and under these azure skies, when the moral conditions are made perfectly right, just as easily, just as honorably, just as beautifully, just as righteously, and a hundred times more scripturally, than on some imaginary, etherial cloud of mystical Swedenborgian dreamland.

The kingdom of Jesus is just like Jesus. For many centuries He was in this world before He became visible on it in a human form. In like manner, His kingdom has for many centuries been unseen as a spiritual force "of righteousness and peace and joy in the Holy Ghost" in the hearts of His true subjects, but that kingdom, like the King, is to come down from heaven and come forth in the first resurrection as a visible body, and displace, according to Daniel, every other kingdom on earth, and occupy the territory. The lives of all the saints, long hidden, will then appear, and all their characters, and prayers, and good works, and variegated graces, and numberless shades and traits of experience, will be openly manifested in cloudless light and unconfused personality. Do we dream of the sweep of this prophetic word, that "our life shall appear" (become visible) when Christ shall appear in His glory? The secret fountains in the soul, the processes of our salvation, our repentances, and consecrations, and prayers, and spiritual struggles, and complex movings and experiences, and stages of growth in grace, and efforts of obedience and charity, will all come forth, in some way, unknown to us, but as well-defined about our personality as the qualities of light are untwisted and hung out in the rainbow on a summer cloud when the storm has passed over.

What is more beautiful in the vegetable world, than a peach orchard drenched with pink blossoms on a lovely spring day? Now, suppose an Icelander, who never saw a peach orchard, were to visit some of our Southern States in the winter, and a fruit grower should take him out to see a large peach orchard, utterly stripped of leaves, with the ground frozen, and all the trees looking like crooked, dead sticks stuck in the ground. On being told that he was looking at a magnificent and valua-

ble peach orchard, he would likely curl his lip in scorn
at the ungainly sight. The proprietor might expatiate
eloquently on the value and merits of that orchard, but
the Icelander would see nothing in it. Let the same
traveler from the frigid zone visit that orchard in April
or May, and find it in full bloom, he would feast his eyes
upon a beautiful picture beyond all his dreams. In the
winter the life of those trees is hidden in the roots, and
the roots are hidden in the earth, and the sun was far
away beyond the equator. When the sun returns from
the tropic of Capricorn, and comes toward the North,
then the secret life in those hidden roots rises with the
coming spring, and comes forth in open manifestation,
clothing those seemingly dead, crooked sticks with gor-
geous beauty and flowery robes of grace and color and
fragrance. This is but one of the Creator's mute prophecies of things to come in those sanctified "trees of
righteousness" planted by His own hand in the garden
of grace. The saints are now living in their winter;
and they look insignificant, deformed, and uninteresting
to their fellows, and their life is deeply hidden. But
when Jesus, who is their life, returns, He will bring the
immortal spring morning, and the secret life in His
saints will bloom forth in such colors of glory, of honor,
of radiance, of princely authority, of fragrant love, that
the very angels will shout for joy, the nations of the
world will stand aghast in terrified bewilderment, and
Satan and his demons, abashed and smitten, will hie
them to the abyss for a thousand years, and the saints
themselves will tremble with amazement and adoration
that they should be so honored and loaded down with

glory, like the twigs on orange and coffee trees that bend beneath the weight of their immaculate and odorous blossoms. Then will come to pass the saying that is written, "Who is she that looketh forth as the morning, fair as the moon, clear as the sun, and terrible as an army with banners?" That is when Jesus "shall come down into His garden, to see His fruit trees in the valley, and to watch the branches of the true vine to flourish, and to see the pomegranates bud with their beautiful red bell-shaped flowers." Song of Solomon 6:10-11. Thus the heavenly life is above nature, but not contrary to nature as God first created it. It is a hidden life, but not a powerless or inactive one, but most full of Divine energy. And it is a life that is to come forth in a most perfect revelation of beauty and glory, "at the appearing of the Lord."

CHAPTER II.

At the time we are passing through any phase of Christian experience, it is difficult for us to understand or to classify the events and phenomena of our spiritual life. But after we get through, we can look back through the medium of an illuminated mind, and mark the steps and the processes in such a way as to lend a helping hand to others who have not yet passed over the journey. The various steps that a soul takes from the time of its conversion to its establishment in the fullness of the Spirit may be described as follows.

1. There springs up in the heart of the young Christian a general desire to grow in grace. His views of growth are vague and as he looks forward upon the Christian journey, a silver mist hangs over the distant horizon, and he catches but faint glimpses of the distant mountains which he is to scale by the grace of God. He does not apprehend clearly the hindrances in his own nature to spiritual progress, nor does he apprehend in any definite way the promises which are made in the Bible of the fulness of salvation. But there is an abiding desire and purpose in his heart to get better, to increase in faith, and hope, and love, to become stronger and more useful. But his whole thought and feeling are characterized by indistinctness.

(22)

2. After awhile there comes to his apprehension the special need of some grace or virtue in which he seems to be lacking. Amid the daily vicissitudes of life, and the ordinary trials, and annoyances, and temptations, and besetments which hem him around, he is made to feel that he needs some special grace by which he can get a more easy victory in daily life. Sometimes it may be a deep sense of the need of a forgiving spirit, or of being more humble, or of being very patient, or of being more self-possessed, or of having a special strength in faith, or love, or calmness of spirit. One person will feel the need of one particular grace more than others, and another person will have a special sense of lacking some other grace. But there will come in some way, a pinching sense of need on the line of some one of the fruits of the Spirit.

3. The next step in the experience will be the soul's discovery that there is an internal hindrance in the heart to the very grace it is seeking after. This is the way in which the Spirit leads the soul to discover the great under-world of the latent carnal mind. And many a Christian, who could not believe at first that he had the remains of inward sin in him, is led to make that discovery, by finding that something in his nature lies right in the way of his progress in grace, and strangles his peace, or joy, or liberty. God works on a scheme of indirections, or in a circuit of truth. This is the way he works in nature, in the currents of the sea, and the blowing of the winds, and the circuits of electricity, and in the laws of the mind. Thus he works in the realm of grace. The believer had his eye on

obtaining some rich and beautiful graces, and pursued it with zest, but in that pursuit he found the barriers to obtaining it within his own heart. And thus the Holy Spirit has led him to search into his inner nature by the indirect route of hunting for some golden grace of which he sees his need. If a Christian in his early love should be told that the reason he cannot grow faster in grace is because he has various forms of evil in his heart, he would not believe it. But in the pursuit of higher degrees of love he is driven back to search the foundations of his heart in a manner which nothing else could have made him do.

4. While making this introspection in his affections and tempers to find out what is the particular besetting evil that prevents his growth in grace, he makes a great discovery that well-nigh horrifies him. He finds that instead of having *one* besetment which checks his Christian progress, there is a whole world of carnality in his nature. These outcroppings of one or two evil propensities, which at first attracted his attention, were only like the mineral veins of a mine, they lead down into a dark region of corruption and blindness, and unbelief, which he hitherto did not dream was in him. Then he begins to understand that the whole body of sin as an evil principle, remains in his heart. This for the time being saddens his spirit, and causes a real grief in his soul. The very fact that he is born of God, and desires to love him more, causes him inexpressible sorrow of heart to find that his whole being is pervaded with a latent yet positive evil. He then begins to see that many of his good deeds, and much of his Chris-

tian work, was tinged with selfishness, or subtle pride, or ambition, or a strain of vanity, or was mixed up with duplicity and double mindedness. This brings on the stage of what has been called the repentance of believers, that is, real grief over inward sin.

5. Next there comes to this soul a thirst for the fullness of Scriptural purity. At first he began with a sense of the need of some one particular grace, but now he sees that he needs a universal cleansing, not only from one form of evil, but from every variety of pride, and unbelief, and selfishness in every form. The light of the Spirit is now widening in the horizon, and he sees that he needs something far more than to be sanctified in spots, his vision takes in the length and breadth of his whole nature, and sweeps the extent of his whole life. Now he yearns for nothing short of a complete and universal cleansing.

6. The next step in this process is, he begins to enter the region of entire yielding of self up to God. Not in the same way that he yielded to get pardon. This is a more profound and interior giving of himself over unlimitedly to the will of God. It is an itemized giving up, of point by point, and thing after thing, in his outward life, and inward life, a letting go of things in the past, and then in the future, and a resigning of circumstances, and plans, and hopes, and anticipations, into the will of God. It is a yielding up of the inward affections, and day dreams, and opinions, and sentiments; a turning over into God's hand of the very core of one's life, with all the contingencies, and the outcomes, and the possibilities of that life. Such a yielding up as

this can never be done except under the immediate
guidance and searching illumination of the Holy Spirit.
It is a thousand miles beyond human logic, or the mere
utterance of words. It is a real, living transaction.

7. When this itemized yielding up of the whole inner being to God is completed, then comes the hour of
perfect trust in Jesus as a Saviour, and cleanser, and
sanctifier. This faith has no struggle in it, it is a sweet,
quiet rest in Jesus, a sort of divine, heavenly indifference as to what the outcome may be. Like a sleeping infant dropping its toy on the floor, the soul has quietly
relaxed, and let go everybody and every thing, and
peacefully rests upon the promise of God, which is the
same to it as the bosom of God. Hence the highest
type of faith is not exercise, but a ceasing from exercise,
a supernatural repose in God, and a letting of the Holy
Spirit do his work without having any anxiety to in-
terfere with him.

8. After awhile this soul will make another discovery concerning the Holy Spirit. At first he is fairly
bewildered with the great blesing he has received, and
can hardly see or talk of anything else except the blessing. But after learning certain spiritual lessons, it
comes to recognize in a wonderful way the blessed Holy
Spirit as a divine Person living within. Then he sees
that his life is to take on the form of a most intimate,
thorough and blessed companionship with a divine
Person who lives in his own spirit. From this time on
he does not rely upon any particular form of experience,
but learns to confide in that blessed Comforter out of
whose fullness flows all good experiences. He then

learns to commune with the Holy Ghost as he did not know how to do amid the first bewildering splendors of the sanctified state. He then learns to let the Holy Spirit use him for the glory of Jesus, and instead of trying to use God's grace and God's gifts, he gets into the secret of so corresponding with the inward monitions of the Comforter, and so understanding the mind of God, that he yields himself continually, with great docility and humility, to be utilized by the blessed Holy Ghost who remains in his heart. This is the state that all sincere Christians have intimations of and desires for, but that so few of them seem to fully enter into in this life. But this is the state which is truly apostolical, and it is for all those who will obey God without fear and in humility.

CHAPTER III.

TWO KINDS OF LOVE.

The love of God poured into our hearts by the Holy Spirit is the sum and substance of all true religion, and everything else that belongs to the Christian religion is either a step to this love, or else an effect that flows out from it. Faith would be useless if it did not lead us into a life of love, and all good works and zeal would be useless, and not acceptable to God, unless they were prompted and pervaded by His love. Hence in a comprehensive sense, there is really nothing but love in pure religion. Not only the most of human beings, but a great majority of nominal Christians do not distinguish the difference between natural human love, and the love of God; and yet the difference is just as great as that between the human soul and the perfections of the Divine Being. Natural human love may resemble divine love in many things, for it is a created affection, made in the likeness of the divine, but in order to understand the Spiritual life we need a clear discrimination between these two kinds of love; the one human, the other divine; the one earthly, the other heavenly; the one natural, the other spiritual; the one temporal, the other eternal; the one fallen and full of defects, the other holy and without blame.

(28)

1. In the Greek Testament, the Holy Spirit has given us a strong distinction between these two kinds of love by using two separate words. The term *"philos,"* with its various forms, is the Greek word for natural or human affection, or that kind of love that springs up instinctively from relationship. The word *"agape,"* with its various forms, is the word for divine love, that is, the temper, the disposition, the goodness, the interior heart-feeling of God. It is true the word *"philos"* is used a few times in connection with God to express His love for Jesus, but it is to be understood as expressing a love of relationship for the man Christ Jesus, the parental affection for the humanity of our Saviour. It is also true that in a few places in the New Testament the word *"agape"* is used to express the spotless sanctified affection of human beings for each other, and of love of husbands for their wives, but in such instances it implies that the whole heart of the perfect believer is flooded with the Holy Spirit, and that the natural human love is filled and overflowed with the divine love. With these explanations, the Scriptures make a clear distinction between the two kinds of love, and it is to be regreted that both of these words *"philos"* and *"agape"* are translated by the same word "love," for it prevents the common reader from discerning the peculiar force of God's word, and distinguishing the vast difference between that which is human, and that which is divine. It could be wished that the word *"philos"* was always translated by the term affection, and then every one could get a clear vision of the mind of the Spirit in the Scripture. Every one who goes on the sea, will notice

that when they are near the shore the water is a
muddy or a light green complexion, but as soon as they
get into deep water the color is a dark blue, and so it is
when we read the New Testament. Wherever we find
human love, it is shallow and sometimes earthly, but
when we cross over into that word *"agape,"* we get into
deep water, where the love is clear, and of a deep, rich,
divine blue. Let us take just one sample from Scripture: Jesus saith to Peter, Lovest thou me? Have you
"agape," divine love, for me? Peter saith, "Yea, Lord,
thou knowest that I love thee," *philos;* that is, that I
have human affection for thee. Jesus saith again the
second time, Simon, lovest thou me, *"agape,"* have you
divine love for me? He saith unto Him, Yea, Lord,,
Thou knowest I love thee *"philos,"* having a human affection for thee. Jesus kept using the word that indi-
cated divine love, and Peter kept responding by that
word which simply meant human affection, and so the
third time when Jesus put the question, finding that
Peter would not respond with the *"agape,"* or divine
love, He dropped down to the plain of Peter's soul, and
put the question the third time, Lovest thou me? Using
the word *"philos,"* asking, Have you indeed human affection for me? This seemed to pierce Peter's heart
more than the previous questions, and he said, "Lord
thou knowest that I have human affection for Thee."
That was just before Pentecost; but after Peter was
purified, and filled with the Holy Spirit, he was lifted
from the *"philos"* kind of love, into the regions of
God's feelings and affections, and in his epistle he
speaks of the domestic affections as being spiritualized,

and filled with divine love, and tells us to "have fervent charity," that is "boiling, divine love," "among yourselves."

2. The human affection has its seat in the soul, or the natural mind, but divine love has its seat and operation in the spiritual part of our being. There is about as much difference between our spirits and our souls as there is between our souls and our bodies. Our soul or natural mind is that which opens up through the five senses to the external world, but our spirit is that part of us where lies the God-consciousness, or its inner feeling and intuitions which open up to the things of God, heaven, eternity, and holiness. There are myriads of people in civilized countries, educated, attending the church, reading books, taking active part in the affairs of the world, and intelligent about things of time and sense, but who know nothing whatever of the great spiritual world, and of that deep, hidden world of God's truth, the divine feelings, sympathies, intuitions, discriminations, compassions, harmonies, truths, moral beauties, and scriptural thoughts, which are just as real as, and far more rich and satisfactory than, all the world of matter or physical science, or political power and glory. This vast spiritual world is never opened to any human being except by the great miracle of grace so awakening, purging, and illuminating the spiritual part of man's being. Just as the scientist, the poet, the mathematician, can look down on the lower animals, and say, "Poor things, if you only knew the glory of this world of mind, and intellect, and figures, circles, colors, and measurements, how happy

you would be," so the saint, filled in his inner spirit with
the light and presence of the Holy Ghost, can look down
upon poor worldlings, philosophers, politicians, and say,
"O, poor things, if you only knew the purity, the tranquility, the interior brightness, vastness, sweetness, and
divine personalities that I see, and enjoy, and repose
in, how happy you would be." Thus as the human affection pervades the natural fleshly feelings, so the divine love pervades and possesses the spiritual nature,
and flowing out through it governs the whole being.

3. The only way we can enter into either of these
kingdoms of human or divine love, is by being born into
it. People often speak of "joining the church," but in
reality nobody ever can "join" the true church of Jesus,
for the natural way to get into it is by being born into it. Our children do not join our families, but they
are born into them; and so the only door-way into either
the Christian church or kingdom of heaven, is by being
born from above of the Holy Spirit. Love is what ought
to be the normal feeling, or the living out-flow of any
nature; for instance, the life of the rose is poured forth
in its perfume, which may be defined as the natural affection of the rose. It is a fact that every bird, or beast,
or living creature, has a specific normal out-flow of feeling, emotion, or affection, which is the expression of
its nature, and there are as many kinds of natural affection as there are kinds of nature in creation. Now,
the only way for anything in creation to have the natural affection of a human being, is to be born with a human heart and soul.

In like manner, the only way to have the feeling,

the affection, or out-flowing disposition of the living God is for fallen men to be born again of the divine Spirit into the divine family relationship. Love is by birth, not by evolution or by development, either as regards human or divine love. The dog is the most affectionate animal of all the lower creation, and yet he can only love with a dog's nature. But suppose it were possible for the dog to be born over again, and born a boy, he would then have a human heart, with human love running out in all the higher, nobler, more intelligent channels of a human soul. Thus, unregenerated men and Adam's fallen race may be amiable, affectionate, and possessed with many beautiful and attractive manners and dispositions, yet all their good qualities, multiplied a thousand-fold, and cultured to the finest pitch, can never be divine love, and can never develop into the love of God, or cross over that great gulf that separates between fallen human affection and the spotless love in the divine nature; and it is only when human beings, on the condition of repentance and faith in Jesus are touched with the Holy Spirit, and born into the divine love, that they can ever experience that love which is from God.

4. While there are some likenesses between human and divine love, there are also many contrasts. Human affection, even at its best, is weak, because it is conditioned on so many things in our life as, for example, heredity. Some children inherit very little natural affection, since it depends on education, on environments, health of body and various gifts of intellect; and hence, in thousands of instances, natural affection breaks down.

Divine love is strong and fresh, and when the inward hindrances, such as inbred sin, doubt, and moral fear, are removed from the heart, and it can take entire possession, it turns the inner man into a moral giant of boldness and perserverance. Human affection is not in itself sinful, but it falls an easy prey to the fallen state of the heart, and almost universally is poisoned with selfishness, or greed, with fleshly lusts, ambition or avarice. So that while on the one hand we have beautiful instances of human love, even among the heathen and savages, as well as among the civilized and cultured classes, of unselfish benevolence and sacrifice even to the death, yet, on the other hand, the world is full of scenes where human love is a gigantic instrument of perverted passion and selfishness. On the other hand, divine love, not only introduced in the heart by the new birth, but perfected by the sanctifying baptism of the Holy Ghost, and filling the whole soul, is a constant fountain of compassion, of charity for others, longing to save and bless all mankind, and is always thinking, praying, planning, and going forth in enterprises to lead souls to Jesus, to bless the poor, to purify the church, to evangelize the heathen, to lift up the fallen, to alleviate pain; for when divine love has its normal action through the human soul, its supreme gladness is in giving out for the benefit of others. Human love is soon exhausted, its fountains are not deep enough, it often dwindles into the poor sentiments of good wishes, but nothing more; whereas, divine love has in it a fountain of satisfaction, and can constantly increase, despite poor health, or poverty, or hard work, or bad treatment; and the other

things that often kill out human affection, can become
the occasions for the love of God in the soul to increase,
to deepen and sweeten with marvelous power. We were
originally constituted in Adam to be vessels of divine
love, and the various parts of our compound being of
body, soul and spirit, never reach their normal state till
entirely possessed and governed by the love of God, the
feelings, and dispositions that run out in liquid rivers
of light from the nature of God. Any effort to make
the body or the mind to live right apart from the
pure love of God, is simply legality or bondage to law;
but when divine love becomes the supreme possession of
a man's inner being, his physical and mental being will
harmonize with God's law easily. Thus we need divine
love to purify, elevate, and properly utilize the natural
affections. This is the divine element that St. John
speaks of when he says, "He that dwelleth in love,
dwelleth in God."

CHAPTER IV.

"And they went and came to Moses and to Aaron, and to all the congregation of the children of Israel, unto the wilderness of Paran, to Kadesh; and brought back word unto them, and unto all the congregation, and shewed them the fruit of the land."—Numbers 13:26.

There is a world of instruction in the incidents that are touched upon in this chapter. O, what a world of interest clusters around the action of the Jews. You know they marched from Mount Sinai right straight toward the land of Canaan, and God's design was that they should go right up into the land of Canaan, without crossing the river Jordan; they were to go on the south side of the Dead Sea, so that there was no river at all to cross, only a valley. Kadesh is the name of the place that was on the boundary line, right between the wilderness on one side and Canaan on the other, and when they came up to this boundary line, there they halted; and from the boundary Kadesh they sent out twelve spies to spy out the land, and bring back word again. The word "Kadesh" means holiness. They took a straight line from the time of their conversion for the land of Canaan, and there was no break, there was no positive rebellion until they came to Kadesh, and there

(36)

is where their faith and patience were tested. There the
spies went out and brought back that wonderful report,
of which we have an account in this lesson; ten of these
men bring back a miserable report of unbelief and rebellion and hardness of heart, and two of the men
bring back a minority report of faith and of patience;
but the people, you remember, took sides with the majority, and adopting the majority report they backed
down from entering the land of Canaan, and from that
time they began to wander forty years in the wilderness,
and when they did cross over they did not cross over on
the south side where the valley was, but they had to
cross over on the north side, across the river.

We learn from this thought that when a young convert comes out of Egypt and is delivered from the guilt
and dominion of sin, and receives within him the tastes
of divine love, under proper guidance he will take a
straight line to Canaan, and when he comes to the boundary line of holiness his faith will be tested. Kadesh
will always be the testing point of everyone's faith; and
if the young convert under divine light, with a willing
heart, will go over into Canaan, then he can go over
without crossing the river; he can go over by simply
crossing a valley; but if he draws back like the people
here did and refuses to go over, he may have a long "up-
and-down" life, with many missteps and terrible vicissitudes in his experience, and when he does enter he must
enter through the severe crisis of the crossing of the
river Jordan. In bringing back of the report from the
land, we see here in the report of the ten men the progress of unbelief. In reading this thirteenth chapter

clear through, and then reading the fourteenth chapter, it is amazing to gather up their ideas and see how their unbelief grows at every step. If you want to know the biography and the history of unbelief and see how it can grow and spread, you will see it in these two chapters. In bringing back their report these ten men gave quite a lengthy account of the land, the products, the climate, and the people; but they bring in that terrible word about the giants; the giants are there, and in all the report that these ten men made, they never mentioned the name of God once. What a significant fact that is! When Caleb and Joshua brought in their report they began by bringing in the Lord, and they said, "If the Lord will be with us we will still be able to go." The ten men on the other hand were talking about what *we* can do, *we* are not able, and *we* saw the giants, to whom *we* were as grasshoppers; it is all *we* all the way through, and *us* and *our*.

Their whole attention was directed to the resources of themselves, while Caleb and Joshua looked over themselves and mentioned God. That is so everywhere in the earth. Unbelief! If you have unbelief in your heart it will always behave like these ten spies. It always searches the human side, looks at what *you* can do, what *you* can be, what *you* can develop; ignores the cleansing ability of Jesus and ignores the almighty Holy Ghost. Then from that standpoint their unbelief gets worse and worse as they proceed, until it reaches the point where they take up stones to stone Caleb and Joshua. People say, I am all right, except I have unbelief in my heart. People think unbelief is a kind of sickly thing that doesn't do much harm in the world. The unbelief of these ten men commenced by forgetting to mention God, but it wound up by being murderous. It so turns out that the men who brought in this report, that the very names of these men indicate their character. By looking at the names that these men bore, we get an insight into their inner character, and you never have the key to a man's life until you get the key of his inner character. Then you can unlock the man's conduct. So you take the ten spies that brought in this majority report, and see what their names imply, and here we have got the key-note of their failure to believe. Sometimes when men die they call in a committee of surgeons for a post-mortem examination. We want to hold a post-mortem examination on these ten men, and find out of what disease they died.

The first name is "Shammua." The English of that name is "Fame." Now you see why that man did not go into the land of Canaan. His very nature, the key to his life, his whole inner character, was woven around a central thought of fame. Love of praise, love of notoriety; he wanted to be great in the eyes of men; wanted to make a great show; wanted to see his name in print and have it heralded through the earth; that is why that gentleman forget to mention God when he rose up and made a report of the committee. The fact is, his own name was so great in his eyes that he forgot to mention God, whereas the Bible says, "In the beginning God. . . . ." In the eyes of the world fame is thought to be a virtue. Young men are taught to be famous; they are exhorted to make a big name for themselves.

We love the fame and honor of distinction, of being flat-
tered. Why, there are thousands and millions of people that think it a virtue, and even nominal Christians
think it is a virtue, but the very things that the world
thinks to be great God despises.

The true doctrine of the Bible is that we are to love
and obey God. We are to trust him and let the Lord
make our reputation, our character, our standing. The
love of fame will keep any man in this world out of
salvation. If you want a pure heart, if you want an inner rest of soul, if you want a deep and settled peace of
mind, you must tear from your breast that miserable
itch of hungering for notoriety. If you have a crav-
ing to be famous in your little set, in the little circle
where you are, I want to say that that is nothing less
than the idolatry of worshiping yourself; it is no wonder that such souls die, no wonder that people do not
give themselves up, when the fact is they are hungry
for fame. That is why they cannot trust God. We
must consent to be little and unknown and humble in
order to enter the land of love.

The next man's name was "Shaphat." The English
of that word is "to judge." Mr. Shaphat was a man
whose inner character and disposition was to get on a
throne and put himself up, and be rendering judgment
on all his brothers. He wanted to measure everybody
by himself. He wanted to judge their motives, to
judge their conduct, and thus he was so busy judging
all his neighbors and family acquaintance, that he un-
consciously got into the place of God. God is the
judge; He alone knows; God alone can penetrate a hu-

man soul; He only can turn on the search-light in your moral nature; and yet there are many people in the world that seem to have this disease of sitting in judgment on people. That is what kept that man out of the land of Canaan. People criticise this and that. I was kept out of the blessing of perfect love for some time because of the spirit of criticism, and yet I did not think I had it very bad; but I want to say, friends, before the Lord ever lets us have a clean heart, before ever he takes the burden from our soul, before he gives the baptism of the Holy Ghost, we reach a place where we are willing that all other people should be esteemed better than ourselves.

As long as you are judging others you are taking the place of the Lord. You are sitting in the seat of the Lord, and are doing the work that doesn't belong to you, and the very spirit of judging human beings will forever keep you out of the land of Canaan, the land of rest. We must lay that aside. When you are judging people you are taking the place of God, and He will not allow anyone to take his throne.

The next name was "Igal." The English of that word is "God will avenge." That is a very good name, apparently, but you look at the import of it. The name implies that this man Igal had in him a spirit of resentment and retaliation, but as he does not want to take the responsibility of executing the penalty against his enemies, he hopes God will do it. He is one of those men that think the Lord ought to go around with a club and beat people, and in his heart he wishes the Lord would smite certain ones to death. This name signifies retaliation from God. In other words, this man would retaliate, but he either cannot, or is afraid to, and so he wishes that God would do it. How many times in your life have there been when you have felt, Oh! if God would only kill some people, if God would only burn somebody's house down; I would not dare kill them myself, but somehow I wish that God would kill them! Do you know there is a killing spirit in there? Have you not been tempted, brother or sister; have there not been times in your lives when you have had that spirit in you, although you did not dare to be the executioner, but in your heart you somehow wished God would put some people under the guillotine? I have heard some men say that they wished God would kill all the saloon keepers; and even Martin Luther, before he got sanctified—he was a grand, good man—said once, "What a sight it would be to see the pope and his cardinals hanging in a row." You will find that people have in them that resentment which leads them to feel that they would not like to hurt certain people, but they wish God would. That man Igal could not go into the land of Canaan; and if we have that spirit in us we cannot get into perfect love. It must be given up. We must cast it down. All resentment and all bitterness must be laid aside.

The next man's name was "Palti." The English for this is, "Deliverance of Jehovah." The meaning of this man's name forms the key to his conduct; it means in his case *orthodox indifference;* and so the man said, "The Lord will deliver us." We need not be in a hurry to go up into Canaan, it is the Lord's work." A great many people say, "If the Lord wants to sanctify me, here I am." There is in them that indifferent, don't-care spirit that talks in an indolent way to God, as much as to say, If the Lord wants to do it, let him do it by main force.

Indifference is one of the worst things that the word of God has to contend with. In the temperance cause, in the missionary cause, in revivals of 'religion, there are thousands who are willing to say "Amen," provided they do not have to give their time, or their zeal, or expend any of their strength, their money, or ability for the cause of God. They are orthodox, yet they slumber on, and say, If the Lord wants to save the world, let him do so; if he wants to sanctify us it's all right.

No, friends, we must work with God; we must co-operate with his Holy Spirit. Hence the lazy, orthodox Palti never got into the land of holiness.

The next name is "Gaddiel," which signifies 'Fortune from God." The key to that man's character was, he served the Lord for what he could make out of him. He was hunting for fortune, he was seeking wealth, and was keenly alive to his own well-being, he simply wished God to give him a good fortune. Fortune from God! · He felt as if God's bounty and grace were the only means of piling up his wealth. There are so many of just such people in the world to-day. They look upon God as simply our servant, and so there are thousands who would like to be Christians, provided they could make something by it; and some Christians would like to get into full salvation, provided they could make something by the operation. I have known people to get into certain communities, and join certain churches, simply for the purpose of making gain; denying their conscience, denying their faith, getting away from their convictions, and for the sake of popularity, for the sake of worldly gain, they simply attach themselves to this church, or that, as an instrument of their own honor and glory.

The idea of turning the blessed God into a money-making machine! Yet they did it in Paul's day right under the apostle's eyes. They said "they supposed that gain was godliness"; and I have heard men talk that way, that the more prosperity they have, the more God will bless them. To turn the Lord and his mercy and his love into a convenience for our welfare, and good fortune, is an awful degradation of grace, and if any one simply uses God as a means of having good fortune, and good success, you can't get it. If we ministers seek the doctrine of holiness, in order merely to have a great revival, we will never get it. If we want the mighty power of God on us, simply for the piling up of big collections, we will never get it. Why? Because we are then using the Holy Ghost, the blessed Spirit of God and his Son, as the means of good fortune. And this man died, and was buried in the desert sands, because he simply wanted God to give him good fortune.

The next man's name was "Gaddi." He was worse than Gaddiel. The word gaddi simply means "good luck." Now Gaddiel wanted good fortune from the Lord. He did have some idea of religion; but the man Gaddi just wanted to have "good fortune;" he was simply in for the big thing, God or no God. There is the key to that man's heart. Mr. Gaddi was desirous of success; anything that would be brilliant, taking, popular, successful, he was in for it. He has a great many followers. They will resort to any foolish thing, if it will only bring prosperity. Instead of worshiping God, our loving Lord, how many there are who worship religious success! Give to God your whole heart, whether you succeed or fail. By a careful study of the Bible you will find all through its pages that the grandest saints were those that never had seeming success.

The Hebrew children said, "Be it known unto the king that we will serve no image. The Lord our God is able to deliver us, but if not, be it known unto you, we will not serve your god, even if we die." Brothers and sisters, God will make you succeed in his way, but I want to say, you must get that idea of success out of your minds, die to it, and when you consent to be a failure for Jesus then the Lord can do something with you. And so Gaddi was a man that went in for success, and found eternal failure.

The next man's name was "Ammiel." The name signifies "The people of God." The key of his character was, "Are we not the Lord's people; are we not the descendants of Abraham, Isaac and Jacob, and have we not been predestinated, and so it does not matter if we do not go up into the land of Canaan." He was depending on his election, on God's decrees. We cannot depend upon our church history, but only upon our fidelity to the blessed God. If your soul is not pure I beg of you do not lean on your past religion, or on church membership. Ammiel depended on that and found a grave in the burning sands, and millions who put their trust in decrees will die in a like manner.

The next man's name was "Sethur." It signifies "secrecy," "mystery." The key to his life is this: "Now this going up into Canaan is too deep and too profound for us, and it won't do for us to meddle with any of these deep and profound mysteries." How many there are who think sanctification is so deep and mysterious, and they say you ought never to mention sanctification where young Christians are, that you thereby discourage them. They say you should only mention sanctification in a whisper, whereas the going up into Canaan and the blessed fulness of salvation is a gospel so plain that boys and girls can take hold of it. There is no great mystery in believing Jesus, and children can be converted and boys and girls can be fully sanctified. Never hold back because you think a thing is a mystery and profound. The greatest profundity in the world is the unbelief of the human heart. Sethur was a secret society man, who thought Canaan must be taken by "grips" and degrees.

The next man's name is "Nahbi," which signifies "to hide," to cover up, to shun, to run away, to conceal one's self. The secret of that man's heart was, he was a coward. He would get behind the tree when the bullets flew, and he would run when he was not being looked at. He did not want to bear any responsibility. He was afraid to take front rank, he was afraid to stand up and be a target for Jesus. He shunned responsibility. What a large family of relatives that man has! People say, Please get somebody else, I am not adapted to it; people who excuse themselves are trying to conceal and to hide. They have the spirit of cowardice. That man could not go into Canaan. It takes a brave heart to come out for the fulness of salvation. It takes a brave heart to come out for Jesus. Brothers and sisters, you must be brave, and if you have any timidity, settle it to die to it. Come to the crucifixion and get the blessed God to take all the cowardice out of you.

The next man's name was "Geuel." He was a high churchman. The name Geuel signifies "The majesty of God." The key to that man's heart is: everything must be done majestically. There must be tone, splendor and dignity about everything. Everything was pervaded by the word majesty. God is majestic. He wants us to give him the majesty, but man's idea of majesty is just the opposite of God's. When we put on majestic forms and ceremonies we only cloud ourselves. And so in all these men you will find the progress of self-love. Begin at the top and run down; it is self. The first word is self-praise; the second is self-enthronement; the third name is self-revenge; the fourth is self-seeking; the fifth name is self-interest; the sixth is self-sufficiency; the seventh is self-security; the eighth is self-deceit; the ninth is self-preservation, and the tenth is self-splendor. You find there is a progress of self-love, and all these men when they came back, and made their report, they put in their report such expressions as: We saw; we saw the giants.

Now take the report of the other two men. The name "Caleb" signifies a dog. The name Joshua signifies salvation. Put the two together, a dog and salvation; the name of Caleb signifies the extreme weakness and helplessnes of the human side. Caleb's name signifies the man's side, so blind, so helpless, so good-for-nothing; and the name Joshua supplements it, signifying God's ability, His grace, that He can cleanse, can save; and you have one name representing the absolute frailty, weakness, depravity of the human race, and the other name signifying the sufficiency of the blessed God to cleanse and save. When the man's side opens and says Lord, I faint, I faint, I am nothing more than a dog; when a man opens his heart without any whitewash in it, without any splendor or self at all, and makes a complete confession to God, Jehovah opens his heart and says to him, I have got salvation; I have got grace; I can forgive; I can purge. When a man confesses everything there is in his heart God will turn around and confess everything that is in His heart. If you will just take the place of a poor little animal, and open your heart to God, he will open his heart of salvation to you.

These two men, when they brought their report, the Bible says, "they brought a report as it was in their heart." The ten men brought a report as it was in their head, and they said, we saw this, and we saw that. But the two men brought their report not as it was in their head, but "as it was in their heart." If you look at God through your head you will be like the ten men; but after you see him in your heart you will get down to the great things of God. When you come to seek the perfection of love don't go head-foremost but go heart-foremost. You do not understand perfection, but God does. Those men lived once. When they lived they had life like we have it, but they are dead and gone. The bones of these ten men are bleaching today, are somewhere in the great Arabian desert,, and the Bible says they fell in the wilderness; but the bones of Caleb and Joshua are reposing this very minute in the land of promise. We will soon be gone; we have not long to live. Let us believe God, and report the precious things of his kingdom, his forgiving, his restoring, his cleansing, his healing, his touch of flaming love, as we see them in our hearts. Compare Numbers 13:28 with Joshua 14:7.

CHAPTER V.

One of the strongest proofs that the Bible is the infallible Word of God, is the fact that its delineations of the soul, and every variety of character so perfectly corresponds with the inward conditions and operations of the human heart, both in sin and in holiness. The Holy Spirit always works in souls exactly according to His own pattern, which He has set forth in Scripture. There are several places in the New Testament where we have a kind of a portrait of spiritual experiences which go to make up a full Christian character and life. One of these passages is found in the first five verses of the fifth of Romans. In the first verse we have justification, and in the second verse sanctification, and in the third, tribulation, and then through the remainder of the text the outworking by various steps of a mature life in the love of God. The subject of sanctification has been so fully and ably written upon by many in recent years, that most who read this book may be familiar with that matter. But there is a field of experience in the outworking and maturing of the life of sanctification that has been comparatively neglected by spiritual writers. Hence, in this exposition we want to allow sufficient space for the first and second verses, and take more time for the unfolding those deeper processes of grace which are subsequent to the first entrance upon the Canaan or heavenly life.

1. The subject in the first verse of the passage under consideration is that of *justification by faith.* In order to better understand this subject we must remember that the Scriptures teach four kinds of justification. The saintly John Fletcher wrote a very able essay upon these four kinds of justification over a hundred years ago, but his wonderful writings were unfortunately brought out in connection with the great theological controversies of his times, which have hindered them from the circulation they merited. We have space only to briefly outline this branch of our subject. Remember that justification covers a larger ground than sanctification, for it must begin previous to sanctification, and run on through all the life of faith, and extend out into all the actions of life, and it culminates when the believer is judged at the second coming of Christ, and stands forever acquitted by the rewards given by the Savior. To justify in a human court is to prove one's innocence. But to justify by grace, is to confess the guilt and be acquitted through the merit of Jesus, who was the sinner's substitute on the cross. The first justification is that by which all the infants of the human race are fully acquitted of any guilt from the sin of Adam. It is true that all infants begotten of a human father are born with a fallen, sinful nature, but there is not imputed to their account any guilt or any action from Adam. This is the kind of justification Paul speaks of when he says, "That as by the offense of one, judgment came upon all men to condemnation, even so by the righteousness of one, the free gift came upon all men unto justification of life." Rom. 5:18. Now you

notice that this kind of justification of infants is universal, it has at one time passed upon all men. And you also observe, that it is without any faith, and without any good works, but "the free gift to every child of our race," because Jesus is the second Adam, and has redeemed all men from condemnation, because of the sins of Adam. Hence, if we now sin, we bring upon us our own guilt, which necessitates another kind of justification.

Now the second justification set forth in Scripture, is by faith alone for the penitent sinner, in which good works can merit nothing. To be justified by faith, is to give up ourselves as utterly lost and undone, and to receive Jesus as our substitute, bearing our death-penalty on the cross, and then the Father remits our sins purely and only on the ground that His Son suffered in our stead. When our sins are pardoned, then the Holy Spirit can regenerate us; for in the nature of things, the new birth could not take place in us till our guilt is removed and we are in a right, a lawful relation with God. Saint Paul writes more upon justification by faith than all the rest of Scripture writers beside.

The third kind of justification is that of the believer after he is saved, and which is by faith and works conjoined. This is the kind of justification that Saint James writes about. It has puzzled a great many people that Saint James, in his epistle, should say, over and over again, that we are justified by works (Jas. 2:14-25). Even the great Martin Luther said that James "wrote an epistle of straw" on the subject of justification. Remember, Luther was just emerging from Romanism, which teaches salvation by penance, and the great reformer did not understand, in his day, the difference between the justification which is by faith in Christ alone, and the subsequent justification in the ongoing daily life of the Christian, which must be proved by good works to accompany faith. Saint Paul elaborates the justification by which we become Christians, and Saint James emphasizes the justification accompanied by good works, by which we prove we are Christians, and continue to be such. Let me call your attention to a very singular thing upon this subject, in connection with Abraham. Saint Paul brings Abraham on the witness stand, to prove that "we are justified by faith alone, without works" (Rom. 4:1-13), and then Saint James brings Abraham on the witness stand to prove "that we are justified by works" (James 3:21). How can they both be true? It is plain enough if you will just consider that Paul refers to Abraham's justification at the beginning of his spiritual life, before he was circumcised; and James refers to Abraham's justification nearly forty years afterward, in connection with his obedience, by which he proved and maintained his justification. So both are true, taken at the stages in Abraham's life to which they apply. Now, do you not see how easy it is for ignorant people to think the Bible contradicts itself, when there is no contradiction?

The fourth kind of justification will be at the second coming of Jesus, when the saints are judged, and their good works will be examined, not for the purpose of saving, but for the purpose of rewarding. This is the kind which Jesus refers to in speaking of the judgment, "by

thy words thou shalt be justified, or by thy words thou
shalt be condemned." When we pass that last great
justification at the judgment-seat of Christ, and hear
our Savior-Judge say, "Well done," that will be the last,
and the everlasting justification of the soul.

Now, you see the first justification of infants, is
without any faith and without any works, and relates to
the soul's exemption from the guilt of Adam's transgres-
sion. The second justification—that of the penitent—
is by faith alone, and relates to our own actions—the
pardon of our personal offences. The third justification
is that of the saved believer, and is by faith and works
combined, and it relates to the obedience of a child of
God. The fourth justification is by works alone, for
only works are mentioned in the judgment, and this justification has reference to rewards for service. Thus,
justification is a larger subject than many suppose.

2. *Sanctification.* The apostle says that after being
justified by faith, and having peace with God, there is
more to follow: "By whom also (that is, in addition to
pardon) we have access by faith into this grace (that is,
the sanctifying grace), wherein we stand and rejoice, in
hope of the glory of God." It is true, the word sanctification is not found in this verse, but that special "grace"
is described as standing firm, or being rooted in Christ,
and in the joy and hope of the glory of God which is to
be revealed. The special feature of sanctification to be
noticed in this verse is, that it is "by faith," just the
same as the penitent's justification is by faith. The
word "access" indicates a doorway. There is no entrance way into true sanctification except by simple

faith in the all-cleansing blood of Jesus. Growth simply enlarges and unfolds a life, or a principle, but does not purify. The growth of a child does not cure it of hereditary disease. In like manner, the growth of a Christian, in and of itself, can never purge out the carnal nature. Good works cannot sanctify the heart, for in that case salvation would come through human action instead of being a divine gift. Thousands of Christians have tried in various ways to get rid of the evil in their hearts by will-power, by growth, by good works, by sufferings, by repression, by sacraments, by gradual processes, but never has one entered into the calm, sweet rest of heart purity, except by the access or doorway of faith as mentioned by Paul. When all the soul's resources are exhausted, and it comes to a place of perfect, everlasting abandonment to the will of God, and faith simply takes the Word Divine as a literal fact, that "our sanctification is God's will," and that "the blood of Jesus Christ cleanseth us from all sin," then the Holy Spirit, in a moment, brings it to pass. Justification removes our actual sins, and sanctification purges out our native heart sinfulness. Justification takes us out of Egypt, and sanctification takes the lingering principles of Egypt out of us. In justification we cross the Red Sea, but by sanctification we cross the Jordan, into Canaan. The heavenly life is the Canaan life, and hence, you see, we do not enter,in a very true sense,the heavenly life, till our hearts are made pure and the Holy Spirit brings us into the fruitful region of pure or unmixed religious love.

3. *Tribulation,* and its outworking in the sanctified

life. "And not only so, but we glory in tribulation also, knowing that tribulation worketh patience, and patience experience, and experience hope, and hope maketh not ashamed, because the love of God is shed abroad in our hearts by the Holy Ghost which is given unto us." No flower ever unfolded to the light of the sun more beautifully than these various words describe the unfolding of the successive forms of experience in the sanctified life. The saints of the Lord will be astonished to find a perfect photograph depicted in the order of these various words, of the lights and shadows, the joys and sorrows, the conflicts and conquests, and all the various problems in their hidden lives. Let us take time to examine each of these words separately, and see how precisely they find an echo in our experiences.

"Tribulation." The word signifies a flail, or threshing instrument, for beating the chaff from the pure, ripened grain. Remember, chaff is not a type of inbred sin, for it is something that is essential to grain in its milk state, and when growing. In a field of growing corn, Scripture compares the heart to the ground, and the growing grain to Christian life, and weeds and briars to carnal affections; but the chaff, or husk, that envelopes the grain, represents those things in us which are essential in the infant stages of grace, but are found useless, and can be threshed away when the believer has reached Christian perfection. When the soul is first sanctified it lives for a period in a sort of heavenly honeymoon, which is distinctly set forth in the old Jewish law, providing that when a man married a wife, he was to be exempt from all public and military duties and

hardships for one year, that he might live in undisturbed
domestic joy. But after that, he must expect to take up
the toils and trials of warfare, and, as Paul says, "endure
hardness as a good soldier." That old Levitical law is
the exact thought of this passage, that after the marvelous joys and bounding heavenly delights that come with
the baptism of the Holy Spirit, that in due time the soul
will be led by one way or another, under the *tribulum,*
or flail, that its chaff, which is now no longer needed,
may be threshed away. After men grow the grain, and
the baptism of warm sunshine has ripened and hardened
it, then the husks, the straw, the chaff, is threshed from
it, that it may be exported to distant markets. In like
manner, when the believer has been purified and solidified, by the warm baptism of the Holy Ghost, there are
many religious or mental infirmities, which need to be
threshed out of him, to prepare him for exportation to
the New Jerusalem. Please notice the following things
as indicating what we may put down as the chaff, which
many Christians have to get cured of after their sanctification. They are not of the nature of inbred sin, but
of human weakness, and ignorance: *Human theology.*
There never was a sanctified Christian that did not have
to cast off some old narrow theology for broader truth.
Rash judgments. Almost invariably souls, young in
sanctification, form judgments of people and things too
quickly. *False zeal.* Every old saint, on looking back,
can see how he used to let his pious zeal run ahead of his
knowledge. *Using slang.* How many hundreds of good,
sanctified people have a habit of using slang, and pun-
ning on words and names that often is like dead flies in

the ointment. *Vacillation.* This is a weakness in the will power, and often lingers with good people after sanctification. *Severity of manner.* Multitudes of souls who are sanctified have a harshness in their words and manners, to the great detriment of their usefulness. *Touchiness.* This is that mean weakness that Mr. Wesley was constantly urging professors of holiness to avoid. *Imprudence.* Many sanctified people lack sense and discretion, and have to learn many things by hard thumps. *Business negligence.* Some of the greatest lights in promoting scriptural holiness are very poor financial managers, and get in debt, or neglect business details, and have to be threshed into business sense. *Fun.* How many have crippled their experiences by giving way to fun, wit, sarcasm, until it was whipped out of them. *Precipitation,* or going too fast, or *indolence,* going too slow, have hindered many. These and many other things of a similar nature, are to be corrected by trials and rebukings, and humiliations, and hardships. The heart is washed from sin by the blood of Jesus, but the head is chastised from its narrowness and foolishness by a rod. You must not confound the washing of the heart with the teaching of the head. You cannot find a word in all Scripture about God washing the head. The Scriptures make no mistake, and they locate sanctification for the heart, and tribulation for the head. Divine providence can always find an appropriate thing to serve as a flail. He may use loss of property, or loss of friends, or health, or sore temptations, or persecution, or ostracism, or sore disappointment, or the misunderstanding of good people, or the bitter hatred of bad people, or things in the outer life, or things in the inner life, to become a flail, that beats away, either steadily or by spells, day after day, or week after week, or month after month, and sometimes for years, till all the graces are inured to trial. Sooner or later, all the principles that were involved in our entire consecration, have to be brought out and tested in some furnace, that they may be proved for the everlasting kingdom.

Separating the elements of chaff is not a cleansing, but a threshing, and, mark you, men never thresh grain while it is in the green, milk state, but only when the grain is grown and pure, and able to bear it.

"Tribulation worketh patience." This word "patience" should be, more properly, "endurance." Tribulation, or threshing, produces in the soul a hardihood, a toughness of fibre, so that it can endure all sorts of things with ease and calmness and sweetness of spirit. When the threshing first begins, the soul, though pure, is tender, and not accustomed to hard usage; but tribulation produces a heroic toughness. There is a youthfulness, a tender childhood, in the sanctified experience, just as truly as in the early days of our conversion. Occasionally, we come across some well-meaning preacher, or evangelist, who lacks knowledge in expounding divine things, and such persons sometimes unwisely present the first entrance into sanctification as being so perfect as to make it appear that every one who is pure in heart will be strong enough never to get wounded, or to get their feelings hurt, or keenly feel the thrusts of the adversary. This, says Mr. Wesley, is too strong. It is unscriptural. The passage we are considering teaches us that it is not the cleansing of the heart that makes the soul tough, but that it is a result of tribulation. Many a purified Christian has keenly felt the mean, unkind thrusts of dear relatives, of carnal preachers, and of those from whom they had a right to expect better treatment, and while they were free from resentment or bitterness, they have bled from many a stab, and in their secret chambers have poured out their feelings of loneliness, and perplexity, and distress, to the blessed Jesus, who is touched with the feeling of our infirmities, and was in all points tempted as we are, yet without sin (Heb. 4: 15, 16). There are two kinds of sensitiveness: One is that mean trait of "touchiness," which takes offense at every slight or rebuke, and cannot bear to be corrected; but there is another kind which is simply a sense of injustice and unkindness, which is normal in any pure nature. Now tribulation will so toughen the tender, sensitive part of the soul as to make it endure injuries, unkindness, and ill-usage of all sorts,so that it is not disturbed, but kept in a holy indifference as to how it is treated. If you take a stick and begin to beat the palm of your hand, in a few moments your hand will feel sore; but if you will give it a rest, and then beat it some more, with another resting spell, and keep up the process at intervals day after day, your hand will get hard and horny, so that you would hardly feel the piercing of a needle in it. That is exactly the thought expressed in this Scripture, that tribulation worketh endurance, or the flail produces toughness.

Remember, in all this threshing, God does not mean to injure your soul, but to separate from you some weakness, or error, or indiscretion, or excess, or foolishness, or babyishness, which sticks to you like chaff to rice, and of which you are perhaps not aware. You are precious to your Redeemer, and He loves you, and the chastening rod is a necessity to knock off some tight-fitting chaff. But, thank the Lord, the flailing will stop when the end has been accomplished. Isaiah refers to this when he says, that "the grain is threshed with a threshing instrument, and the fitches are beaten out with a staff, and bread corn is bruised, because he will not ever be threshing it." Isa. 28:27, 28. At last the saint gets into a place where nothing hurts him, and he can "endure all things" with a sweet and patient spirit, and, in fact, pay no attention to a thousand injuries that used to greatly distress him.

"Patience worketh experience." That is, toughness produces a deep inward knowledge of ourselves and the things of God. The Greek word rendered "experience" signifies "to prove," to demonstrate, to put things to a test. Our English word experience is made up of three Latin words—*ex* (out from), *per* (yourself, your personality), and *science* (knowledge, or wisdom); that is, "experience" means knowledge, certainty, assurance, that you have acquired out of the depths of your own heart. Thus the spirit of endurance causes each Christian soul to search itself, the Bible and God's providence, and in secret prayer, in solitary meditations, to get acquainted with God, to prove His promises, to learn His ways, and to solve the great problems of life, all alone in the school of trial, till it comes forth as from a divine university, educated more thoroughly in immor-

tal knowledge than all the schools of earth could have taught it. The word "experience" not only means knowledge, but compound knowledge, knowledge that has been doubled by first going down into the heart, and then being wrought out in little details under manifold testings. Saint John refers to this double, or compound knowledge, when he says, "We do know that we know him." 1 John 2:3.

"Experience worketh hope." This word "hope" refers to a bright outlook and anticipation of good things to come at the coming of the Lord. In certain localities, especially in Scotland and New England, many people use the word "hope" in an improper sense to mean the new birth. They will speak of "getting a hope" when they refer to getting religion, or being pardoned. Such is not the meaning of the word hope in the New Testament. In Scripture the word "hope" refers to something in the future that we are firmly depending upon. The apostle distinctly says, "What a man seeth, why doth he yet hope for?" Now, out of religious experience—that is, if it be properly accompanied with Bible knowledge,—there will spring forth a beautiful and strong expectation of receiving that vast inheritance promised to the overcoming believer. Did you ever count over the numerous things that are promised in Scripture to the overcoming saints? There is "victory over death," or if Jesus comes sooner than death, the promise of "translation" and "rest in Paradise," and a place in "the first resurrection," and in "the marriage supper of the Lamb," and then the "coming again with Jesus" to "rule the nations" for a thou-

sand years, and to "inherit the earth," and to "be kings
and priests," and to "sit with him in his throne," and
to have "authority to judge the world," and "to judge
the angels," and to have "a mansion in the city of pure
gold," and "to see the face of God," and "to know as we
are known," and to be everlastingly free from sorrow,
or pain, or ignorance, or whatever causes tears. Everyone of these items is pledged to the overcoming saint
by multiplied promises in the Word of God. This is
the vast field over which hope hovers.

"And hope maketh not ashamed." A soul full of divine hope is buoyant, cheerful, brave, not discouraged
by things in the past. This is the spiritual biography,
sketched out by the apostle in these five verses. But the
secret of the whole process is in the last clause—"Because the love of God is shed abroad (or poured into)
our hearts by the Holy Ghost." The Holy Spirit is the
divine agent that pours into us the love of God. It is
divine love poured into us that works out the great
process. Tribulation would bruise us to death, if it was
not that the love of God, like a lubricating oil, was
poured into our hearts. And endurance would never
work experience, if it was not pervaded and possessed
with the love of God. Thus, at every step of the way, it
is divine love poured into us by the Holy Spirit, that
forms the true Christlike character, which will be the
golden grain gathered into the everlasting kingdom of
our Lord.

CHAPTER VI.

PROOFS OF HUMBLE LOVE.

It is one of the characteristics of the spiritual age that God does not always reveal to a devoted soul the progress it is making, for the very reason that if the soul knew of all its advanced steps it would often hinder the progress itself. So the Holy Spirit lovingly conceals his own work oftentimes in order that by a sense of poverty the soul may be pushed on to a swifter growth. Then there are other times when the Holy Spirit has got the believer upon some elevated point he will give him a view over the spiritual landscape, that he may see what God hath wrought and be still encouraged to higher attainments. But right amid the wear and tear of Christian life there are certain proofs which we may test ourselves by as to whether we are in a state of perfect crucifixion and in unbounded divine love. The love of Christ in us must not only be severely tested, but every advancing degree of that love will be tested. Among these proofs we may mention the following:

1. To have the love of God in a state of pure faith—that is, to be able to discern in our spiritual nature that we love God with all our hearts, even apart from all pleasant sensations in the emotional nature. There are three kinds of emotion—bodily, soulish and spiritual; and if apart from all happy, nervous conditions, and

apart from all exhilarating feelings in the mental or soulish nature, we can be conscious in the deep inner spirit that we prefer God and love him above all things in the universe, we may know that we are in a state of pure love.

2. Another proof of humble love is to accept of outward poverty as a gift from God, and, in great meekness of spirit, not only be willing to be poor, but even to be the object of charity, and, if come to that, be a charity patient in a hospital—to take the place of Lazarus at the rich man's gate, and become an object of the charity of others, even when they do not especially love us, but to be so united to God's will that we see through all secondary agents, and look to God alone, and receive the most humiliating circumstances of life as an expression of God's will and love, with meek and quiet spirit—this is a proof that the heart is perfectly crucified and full of lowly love.

3. To have our most sacred faith denounced and treated with contempt; to have our prayers scoffed at, our deepest experiences treated with contumely and scorn; to have our fellowship with the Holy Ghost ridiculed, not only by sinners but by professed Christians and ministers; to have our testimony to the precious blood criticized and denounced as a delusion; to have our motives impugned and grossly misrepresented even by other professing Christians; to have our faith in the great old doctrines of the Bible, of heaven and hell, of future rewards and punishments, of the three adorable persons in the Trinity, of the hope of the coming of Jesus and his reign on the earth, of the virtue of his

blood, of healing diseases; to have all these dearest be-
liefs of the heart set at naught by chief priests and professed friends, and yet to be so thoroughly crucified as
to be undisturbed and to keep in a still, patient, loving disposition, without contention, without agitation—
this is a proof of humble love.

4. Another proof of a real humble spirit is to have
the natural affections cut all to pieces by harsh words,
unkind treatment, or mangled by scorn and neglect, and
for the soul to seek no consolation from the creature,
but to give itself up to God in unlimited abandonment
and seek only the solace that comes from the blessed
Jesus. Unless a soul is thoroughly crucified and in a
state of divine union, it will, under such circumstances,
when its natural affections are bruised and disappoint-
ed, turn to some creature for comfort; it will go to old
friends, or to supposed friends, to seek for help; it must
unbosom its woes to somebody, for counsel and sympathy. And although such a soul may be a Christian,
yet, if it is not in perfect union with God and in sweet
intimacy with the Holy Spirit, where it understands how
to draw all its comforts from God, it will invariably turn
to some creature. But if it can quietly turn to God
alone for consolation, that is a proof of its perfect humility and love.

5. There are times when the true believer passes
through states of mind or experience which resemble a
great western blizzard, where the wind seems to blow
from every quarter at the same time, and the snow is so
blinding that you cannot see your way. In such cases
there will be the most contradictory vicissitudes. Good

things and bad things seem terribly misplaced, as if good and evil had changed places and wore each other's faces and garments; where divine providence seems unhinged and where infinite mercy seems to be tantalizing the heart. Now, if the soul can shut its outward eyes and with the interior vision of faith look right through the tangled mass of such vicissitudes, and discern God in it all, and anchor itself to his pure will in a holy defiance of the appearance of things, and have just the same confidence in God and his word then as in fair weather, that is a proof of a state of humble love.

6. To work for God through months or years and be the instrument of accomplishing what seems to be a good work and then to have it all torn into rags and seemingly destroyed from the earth without losing heart, without getting religiously vexed, without ever charging God unkindly, but to lean back on him and keep gentle and full of peace, is a proof of self-renunciation and pure love. It is a singular trait of good people, even very religious people, even those professing full sanctification, to become wonderfully attached to their own work, and when they have accomplished something for God they unwittingly love their work and make a saintly idol of it. Then when God allows the precious thing to be torn to pieces they feel smitten to the dust, because they loved their holiness work instead of fixing all their love on the dear Lord alone. This is why divine Providence allows so much of Christian work to go to wreck, for he is determined that not even the best of things shall take his place in our love. Now, if you can work for God, and yet keep your heart entirely weaned from

your work, so that you can see it blow to pieces with a
sweet happy spirit in God alone, that is a proof that you
are dead even to your righteous self, and that Christ indeed lives in you and that you have his meek and lowly
spirit.

7. To sow and have others reap is a proof of humble
love, especially if you can see them reap with the same
thankfulness as if you did your own reaping. It will put
a Christian's love to a real test to cordially embrace this
truth. To toil through summer's heat or winter's cold,
to give line upon line and precept upon precept without
seeming to produce adequate results; to exhaust our resources in boring a well for oil and get within one foot
of the vein when the last penny is gone and then to have
some one else take the well and bore only a few inches
and strike a fortune of oil, and even rejoice in the
other's good fortune—this is unselfishness. Yet all we
need to give us this grace is that immensity of faith to
see that God owns everything; and if we toil for him
without seeing the fruit, and some one else reaps the
harvest—if we really love God with pure, unbounded
love we will rejoice that God is getting the harvest from
some other hands just as much as if he got it from our
hands.

8. Another proof of a lowly, loving heart is to receive all sorts of injuries and unkind treatment without
making any reply, and even making it the occasion for
the exercise of the warmest love and prayer for those
who injure us. I think it is Saint Clemachas who tells
us that he knew of three instances where very good men
received very mean treatment and suffered much injury

from their fellows, and he noted the different degrees of grace manifested by each. In the first case the good man bore meekly all the unkindnesses without any reply, but quietly hid himself in God. In the second the humble man rejoiced that he had an opportunity of suffering for Jesus and with Jesus, so that he went beyond the first case, not only meekly bearing it, but ever rejoicing for the privilege of suffering. In the third case the saint felt such a deep sorrow and sympathy for those who had injured him that he wept for them. He not only had meekness to bear it, as in the first instance, and gladness at the privilege of suffering, as in the second, but his love was so divine and fiery and unselfish that he prayed with loving tears for those who injured him. Now, all of these three men manifested perfect love, but they show the different stages which there may be in the pure love of Jesus.

9. To be in a storm of distress and sorely tempted and tried in manifold ways and yet not to advertise it, but tell it all out to God in secret prayer, and keep a calm, peaceful spirit, and to walk calmly before our fellows, and give them the sunshine even when the heart is bleeding and the mind is perplexed with manifold trials —this is proof of a truly humble, loving heart.

10. To work for God with all our strength, without waiting for happy feelings, even though our spirit may feel dry and sorrowful, but to have a lofty, pure faith that persistently keeps us going without joyful sensations, this is pleasing to God. And a still higher form of this grace is to see others being saved or getting blessed through our ministry, while we work in a dry or sorrow-

your work, so that you can see it ow to pieces with a
sweet happy spirit in God alone, t is a proof that you
are dead even to your righteous se and that Christ indeed lives in you and that you ha his meek and lowly
spirit.

7. To sow and have others rea s a proof of humble
love, especially if you can see the reap with the same
thankfulness as if you did your o reaping. It will put
a Christian's love to a real test to rdially embrace this
truth. To toil through summer eat or winter's cold,
to give line upon line and precep pon precept without
seeming to produce adequate res ; to exhaust our resources in boring a well for oil get within one foot
of the vein when the last penny i ne and then to have
some one else take the well and e only a few inches
and strike a fortune of oil, an ven rejoice in the
other's good fortune—this is un hness. Yet all we
need to give us this grace mensity of faith
see that God own if we toil for
without seei e else reap the
harvest
lov

from their fellows, and he noted the different degrees of
grace manifested by each. In the first case the good man
bore meekly all the unkindnesses without any reply, but
quietly hid himself in God. In the second the humble
man rejoiced that he had an opportunity of suffering
for Jesus and with Jesus, so that he went beyond the
first case, not only meekly bearing it, but ever rejoicing
for the privilege of suffering. In the third case the saint
felt such a deep sorrow and sympathy for those who had
injured him that he wept for them. He not only had
meekness to bear it, as in the first instance, and gladness
at the privilege of suffering as in the second, but his
love was so divine and fierce and unselfish that he prayed
with loving tears for those who injured him. Now, all
of these three men manifested perfect love, but they
show the different stages which there may be in the pure
love of Jesus.

9. To be in a storm of distress and sorely tempted
and tried in manifold ways, and yet not to advertise it,
but tell it all out to God in secret prayer, and keep a
calm, peaceful spirit, and to talk calmly before our fellows, and give them the sunshine even when the heart is
troubled and the mind is perplexed with manifold trials,
is the proof of a truly noble, loving heart.
. . . work for God with all our strength, without
. . . happy feeling . . . though our spirit may
. . . and sorrowful, . . .

ful state, and they are made happy through our sorrow, and well watered through our dryness, and lifted up through our humiliation, and made rich through our poverty, as if they were drawing the very juices of our soul away from us, and yet all the while to have a sweet, God-like contentment that we can spend and be spent for others, this is proof of a genuine apostolic condition of mind.

11. To have God strip us of all sensible comfort, and seem to shower his extraordinary favors upon others, and leave us, as it were, in desolation, and at the same time to load us down with many arduous labors and great responsibilities, while divesting us of what we regard as adequate joys, and yet, through it all, to steadily behold him with the eye of pure faith, and to love him with a deep, pining, quivering love beyond the expression of all words, this is a mark of genuine self-abnegation and holy love.

12. Perhaps the highest proof of humble love is to be able to rejoice when God triumphs at our cost. When we love God so much that we have a real gladness in seeing his will and honor and truth manifested, even though it be at the expense of our loss or our deep humiliation, and even our temporary degradation, this is pure love, and this is the love we must have to please God, for we must have such a deep, all-consuming preference for God that we will take sides against ourselves, despise our own interests, and be willing to tear ourselves down, and rejoice at any defeat which comes to our self-life, and, as it were, utterly desert ourselves and go over and join the victorious legions of God's at-

tributes and make one cause with God in fighting against ourselves. This kind of love has a secret laughter every time the will of God succeeds, and especially when it succeeds against our blindness and foolishness, for we discern that the more we are conquered the deeper is our union with God.

CHAPTER VII.

THE MINISTRY OF SORROW.

Sorrow is the normal state of a world that is fallen, and yet under conditions of redemption. Sorrow on earth is the root out of which can be made to grow and blossom the sweetest joys of heaven. Sorrow in man is his natural capability for the joys of the supernatural. Sorrow is a species of suffering with hope in it. Suffering with no hope in it is despair, and that is the normal condition in hell. On the other hand, joy, pure, boundless joy, without a trace of sorrow, is the normal state in heaven. In the true sense of the word, sorrow is preeminently a thing belonging to this world, because it occupies a middle ground between the hopeless anguish and hatred in hell and the bliss of heaven. Hell is a starless night, and heaven an endless, cloudless noon; but sorrow is a night into which is sifted the silvery light of moon and stars. Sorrow is the pathetic poetry of a fallen world in which hope still lingers. The heavenly life on earth is tinctured all through with many kinds of sorrow. When Scripture says that "sorrow is better than mirth," it is with special reference to life in this world, and not to the life in heaven. There is nothing on earth that is not in some way related to sorrow, or hedged in by it, or that does not partake of its color and tone. We are redeemed by sorrow. Our Savior, in pouring out His precious blood for our everlasting salvation, said, "I am exceeding sorrowful, even unto death." Repentance is made up of many kinds of sorrow. The consecration of the believer is steeped in holy sorrow. Almost all prayer is saturated with various kinds of sorrow. The power of music depends on the sorrow there is in it. The poetry of the great masters, that holds our intellects spell-bound, derives its mighty magic from the sad strains of sorrow that run all through it. It is the sorrow element in everything that seizes and holds the hearts of mankind beyond any other influence. It is sorrow that immortalizes battlefields, and monuments, and tombs, and great heroes, and martyrs. It is the sorrow piled up in the Wesminster Abbey that draws thousands annually to walk through its halls with silent, uncovered heads. It is the sorrow in the Bible that makes it the most natural as well as the most divine book on earth; and kings, philosophers, young men and maidens, beggars and lonely savages in the forest, are more deeply touched with the pathetic lives of the dear old weeping patriarchs than with the shallow, heartless noise of mere fleshly events. Sorrow is the universal language of earth, and more easily understood by human hearts than any other one thing. It is the background of all our brightest joys. The Holy Ghost does not prohibit this element of our nature, but bids us "to sorrow not as those who have no hope." Though sorrow may have an Ethiopian complexion, yet, like the eunuch under Queen Candace, it is a thing of great authority, and has charge of the golden treasures of knowledge and wisdom and everlasting life (Acts 8:27). When sorrow comes under the power of divine grace, it works out a manifold ministry in our lives.

1. *It is the ministry of sorrow to break down hard natures, and melt stubborn wills.* There are men who have plenty of mind, and capacity to see truth, to sanction righteousness, but whose heart-nature seems made of flint. They lack feeling, warmth, tenderness. They look upon religion as a cold morality, or a set of business-like duties, or as a financial and political transaction with God. They look upon religious emotion as weak and womanish, and if they are church members, and make any pretense to religion, they are more like baptized mules than little children with their Heavenly Father. God takes His time, and watches His opportunity, and slowly undermines these tough natures, till some day an uneasy feeling comes up from the fountain of their being and creeps all through them. Calamity takes hold upon them. God allows most bitter disappointment to crush some darling hope, or plan. Clouds gather; misunderstandings, separations, sharp and sudden turns in the intellectual or financial or social life transpire; or health breaks down, or bereavement turns life into a walking cemetery. Then sorrow gets in its beautiful work, and fairly laughs behind its mask of tears at the work it will do. As in the late afternoon, the shadows of the great, rugged mountains stretch themselves across the low valley, as if the proud mountain peaks had knelt down to pray on the dewy meadow in the evening hour, while the stars of evening begin to light their lamps, as if to make a sanctuary of the spot;

so it often happens that sorrow is an afternoon gospel on many a stubborn soul, and gets many a proud heart to bow down in the valley of tears.

2. *Sorrow weans us more effectually* than anything else from many things that prevent our perfect attachment to God and heaven. We are not only all of us chil dren, but we are always children, and always taking on new kinds of childhood. When we drop one form of childhood, we simply take on another kind, or another degree of childhood, on a different scale of life. Children cry for toys, and men have shed tears for failing to get the White House, and Generals have wept aloud on battle fields for not being allowed certain positions of honor, and great doctors of divinity have cried like whipped babies when they failed to get some ecclesiastical toy. No nurse on earth can wean the soul from its old loves, its ambitions, its own good works, its manifold entanglements, like dear, old, dusky sorrow. As mothers pour sweet balm over the chafed limbs of their little children, so sorrow puts a quietness into restless characters, stills the noise, soothes the pain, and works such a revolution that the soul is perfectly content to lose everything and relinquish, let go, give up, and turn away from its dearest idols, its fondest dreams, its strongest ambitions, with a tranquil indifference that is in itself really sweeter than if all its old desires had been gratified. Sorrow over their failures has brought more peace than they would have had if successful. Sorrow is the great power of disenchantment. It takes the veneering from what we thought was solid mahogany. It pulls off the cheap paper that we thought was

some great master's frescoe. It unties strong cords
that seemed to defy every other power.

3. *Sorrow widens the soul.* Nobody ever suspects
the little, mean narrowness in his heart till God's flint
hammers have broken him all to pieces, and scattered
the fragments over the great fields of time and providence. Human biography is filled with instances which
show that the men and the women of great, world-wide
hearts have been those who were the children of deep
sorrow. Proud royalists dug up the bones of Cromwell
and burned them, and scattered the ashes upon the
winds of heaven. They acted in blind hate, but God
saw that the grave was too small to contain such bones,
and from that on, the spirit of civil liberty has been
spreading, as if all mankind had sucked into their lungs
a portion of the ashes of Cromwell's bones, which were
tossed to the universal winds. This is the ministry of
sorrow. It lifts the soul out of geographical lines and
sectarian walls, and contemptible caste, and bitter ra-
cial prejudices, or little, narrow religious cliques, and
makes it a citizen of heaven, a universal lover and friend
of all mankind, and a princely heir of the ages to come.
There is among some narrow Christians a water baptism which pens one up to what is called "close communion." The soul that God chooses to be baptized into
sorrow is made a thousand worlds too large for such
earthly littleness. Joseph had more sorrow than all the
sons of Jacob, and it led him out into a ministry of
bread for all nations. For this reason, the Holy Spirit
said of Joseph, "He was a fruitful bough by a well,
whose branches ran over the wall" (Gen. 49:22). It

was through sorrow his heart grew big enough to run over the Jewish wall, and feed the Gentiles with bread; and now Gentile Christians need a baptism that will lead them over the church walls to love and feed the scattered children of Israel. Sorrow is the Mary that breaks the alabastar boxes of our hearts and lives, in order that the costly perfume may fill the entire house, instead of being pent up. God never uses anybody to a large degree, until after He breaks them all to pieces.

4. *Sorrow reveals unknown depths* in the soul, and unknown capabilities of experience and service. Gay, trifling people are always shallow, and never suspect the little meannesses in their nature. Sorrow is God's plowshare that turns up and subsoils the depths of the soul, that it may yield richer harvests. If we had never fallen, or were in a glorified state, then the strong torrents of divine joy would be the normal force to open up all our soul's capacities; but being in a fallen world, sorrow, with despair taken out of it, is the chosen power to reveal ourselves to ourselves. Hence it is sorrow that makes us think deeply, long and soberly. Sorrow makes us go slower and more considerately, and introspect our motives and dispositions. It is sorrow that opens up within us the capacities of the heavenly life, and it is sorrow that makes us willing to launch our capacities on a boundless sea of service for God and our fellows. We may suppose a class of indolent people living at the base of a great mountain range, who have never ventured to explore the valleys and canyons back in the mountains, and some day, when a great thunder-storm goes careering through the mountains, it turns the hid-

den glens into echoing trumpets, and reveals the inner
recesses of the valleys, like the convolutions of a mon-
ster shell, and then the dwellers at the foot of the hills
are astonished at the labyrinths and unexplored recesses
of a region so near by, and yet so little known. So it is
with many souls who indolently live on the outer edge of
their own natures until great thunder-storms of sorrow
reveal hidden depths within that were never hitherto
suspected.

5. *It is through sorrow the soul learns obedience.*
Scripture tells us that even Jesus "learned obedience by
the things which He suffered." Many have stumbled
over this Scripture. Jesus had in Him the principle
of perfect obedience from His birth, and He never once
disobeyed the Father in thought, word, or act. But
that perfect spirit of obedience had to be brought out
and unfolded in a thousand various applications and
directions, and under all sorts of human limitations and
vicissitudes among those who constituted the world's
sinful society. Now, in the carrying out of His perfect
obedience there were circumstances painful and sorrowful, and through suffering He learned the importance, the true value, and the best way of obedience.
In a similar way, the true child of God finds out
through sorrow the very deepest and most loving obedience. It is sorrow that brings the soul into the Calvary-
life of Jesus, and introduces it into the priestly life of
Christ, that of compassion and sympathy and prayer
for others. As the mordant fixes the colors in a dye, so
sorrow gives fixedness, perseverance, to the spirit of
obedience.

6. *But sorrow will pass away.* It ministers now in the heavenly life, but its ministry will pass away when the curse is lifted from the earth, and the age of glory succeeds to the age of grace. It is in the day when the saints of God shall be gathered at Mount Zion, "with songs and everlasting joy upon their heads, that all sorrow and sighing shall flee away." It is when the Lamb is to gather His redeemed ones in the New Jerusalem, and "lead them by fountains of living waters' that God shall wipe away all tears from their eyes." Sorrow is the pathetic moonlight that in the present dispensation ministers to grace, and brings forth some delicate flowers, that are not strong enough at first to bear the hot sunlight of supernal joy.

CHAPTER VIII.

THE HEAVENLY ESTHER.

Although the book of Esther does not contain the name of God, yet it is filled with his living presence and amazing providence. The characters mentioned in the book are not only historical, but prophetic as well; and throw their startling shadows across the face of the centuries. Let us select from this book the leading characters, and in the light of the New Testament, see if we can trace out their prophetic import. Remember, that Ahasuerus was the monarch of the world, and the events here recorded foreshadow things concerning the true and Rightful Ruler of this world, who is the Jehovah Jesus.

1. The great King, at the close of a festivity, wanted his queen, Vashti, to break the rigid customs of an Eastern harem, and come forth in public society, that the Princes might see her beauty, and perhaps thereby be more strongly attached to the dynasty. There is a shadow in this, that Jehovah, who at first arranged to keep his earthly queen, the Jewish people, in seclusion from all other nations as a great national and secret treasure, wanted them at last to accept of the great gospel feast provided by Christ, and the gift of the Spirit, and at that feast God planned that this Jewish people should now break forth beyond their exclusiveness, and be the Lord's gospel missionaries among all the nations.

2. Vashti clung to her harem prejudices, and utterly refused to break the iron law of caste in which she had been trained. So she proudly disobeyed her husband's command and kept to her seclusion. She preferred to break the highest authority in the kingdom, rather than break down the middle wall of caste and education between herself and the people of the kingdom. How truly this fits in with the iron pride of the Jewish people, in preferring to break with Jehovah, and spurn his commands, in preference to giving up their carnal national pride, or breaking over their Hebrew caste, to be a blessing to the hated Gentiles. Paul speaks of the wall of partition that in his day existed between the proud Jew and the Gentile. God wanted the Jewish race to feast on gospel wine, and under those festive joys, to break over their caste, and be evangelists to the Gentiles, and show forth to the poor heathens those queenly beauties of grace and truth which had for centuries been thickly veiled in the pale of Israel. But the Jews as a people clung to their vail and pride, and exclusiveness, and kept on, like Vashti, despising the common people.

3. For this offense Vashti was put away from being queen, and degraded in the eyes of those who had almost worshipped her. This is exactly what happened to the Jewish people, for by rejecting the gospel, with its world-wide evangelism, Israel ceased to be God's earthly queen, and in the language of their own law, God gave them a bill of divorcement, which will continue until the "times of the Gentiles are fulfilled." And, like Vashti, that queenly nation turning away

from the gospel, went down under disgrace, scattered and peeled, unto this day.

4. Then a call went forth to hunt out among the nations for another queen for the great monarch. How clearly we can all see that this portends the going forth among the nations to gather out the church of the first-born, a holy and elect people, "to be the Lamb's wife," the queen consort of his coming heavenly kingdom. Do not fail to note that a great number of beautiful maidens were gathered out from the nations, but only one of them could be the queen. This is the true teaching of Scripture, that not all the saved ones become the bride of the Lamb, but from among those who are called out from the world, there is a second selection of those who are willing to enter into the baptism of death with Christ, who are to form the Lamb's wife. David speaks of the queen by the King's side, and beside her a great company of virgins who are her companions (Psalm 45:9-14.) The passage, "many called and few chosen," has the meaning of many being saved, while but a few get into the Bridehood company.

5. The young women gathered out for the King were put in charge of the great Chamberlain, to be fed and trained, that in everything they might be rendered noble, attractive, and suitable to adorn the Empire. Of all the maidens Esther won the admiration of Hegai, the Chamberlain, who gave her special care. In like manner all the followers of Christ that are gathered out from the world, are put in the custody of the Holy Spirit, that He may purify, and anoint, and feed, and train them, to be presented to the King. Those believers

who have in them the deep disposition of entire abandonment to God are, like Esther, the most attractive to
the Holy Spirit, and they are the ones the most docile
and obedient to the guidance of the Spirit, and upon
whom the Divine Comforter bestows the greatest discipline and care. Now, just bend your eyes down a little
closer and notice a peculiar trait that distinguished Esther from the other maidens. We are told that "when
every maid's turn came to visit the King, they were allowed to have every desire, as to what they wanted given
to them," and doubtless they plied their wits as to what
gifts they would ask. "But when Esther's turn came,
she had no desire, and required nothing but what Hegai,
the Chamberlain, appointed for her." What a revelation
this is of perfect guileless simplicity and purity of soul.
Those who wanted gifts had mixed motives, and pride,
and selfishness, which is the state of those believers who
still have the love of display, or honor, or place, and are
attached to their gifts and graces. But Esther is a model
of those servants of Christ, who want nothing except
what the Holy Spirit appoints, and whose hearts are
purged from selfishness, or vanity, or the love of gifts,
and who are clad in perfect humility, and in whose souls
there is no guile. These are the ones that are fitted for
the queenly rank in the great kingdom of God.

6. It was at the end of a specified term of probation
that Esther was publicly chosen and accepted by the
Monarch to be his queen, and a proclamation was made
throughout the kingdom. In like manner, at the close
of this dispensation, which from the day of Pentecost is
the church age, at the coming of Jesus to gather his

saints, all the saved ones will be presented by the Holy Spirit to King Jesus, and from among all the millions who are gathered unto him, there will be a special company, whose devotion and spiritual beauty, like that of Esther, will outshine all others, and who will be accepted as the Bride of the Lamb, and clothed with extraordinary rank and authority in the coming age.

7. Soon after the enthronement of young Esther, there began to appear an awful enemy in the person of Haman in the kingdom. This Haman is called the Agagite, and was doubtless a descendant of that wicked Agag that Saul spared but whom Samuel slew, and through all these hundreds of years the family of Agag had sought revenge upon the Jews. So Haman laid a dark plot to have all the Jews slain. He is a fitting type of the beastly Antichrist that is to personally arise among the nations after the Bridehood saints have been caught up from the earth. The apostle speaks of Antichrist "already at work in mystery," but clearly indicates that the presence of the Holy Ghost in believers hinders the Anti-christ coming in person, but when that which hinders is taken away, the saints caught up to the Lord, then that wicked one, the personal Antichrist, will be revealed. (See 2 Thess. 2:3-10.) Thus, as the wicked Haman is revealed after the exaltation of Queen Esther, so the Antichrist will appear after the exaltation of the Bridehood saints to be with the Lord in the air.

8. When Haman's murderous plot was revealed, Mordecai, acting for his people, rent his clothes, and put on sack-cloth, and went out into the city, crying with a loud and bitter cry! Please note the relationship be-

tween the crying Mordecai down in the streets, and the
young queen up yonder in the palace. When the saints
are caught up to meet the Lord in the air, a vast multitude who believe in God, both Jews and Gentiles, will
be left behind on the earth. Under the awful reign of
the beastly Antichrist, the nations will mourn, and especially those who believe in God, but who were not prepared to meet Christ, will mourn in dust and ashes, and
cry like dear old Mordecai, with a loud and bitter cry.
The Scriptures speak of the tribulation of those days, as
surpassing anything of the past, even that of the flood.
It is called "the time of Jacob's trouble," for as Haman
tried to kill the Jews, so the Antichrist will make an
effort to destroy them all. (Jer. 30:6, 7.) That will be
the time of the wailing of the five foolish virgins who
had no oil, that is, foolish Christians who will not have
the Holy Spirit.

9. Queen Esther, breaking through all rules of eti-
quette, took her life in her hand to plead for her people,
and for the overthrow of Haman. It requires just such
a spirit of martyrdom in the hearts of saints to qualify
them for a place in Christ's Bridehood. Let us not
think that the life of prayer stops with the believer
when he dies, or is caught up to the Lord, for Scripture
denies it. Jesus has passed beyond death, but his great
life of prayer goes on. John positively affirms that he
saw into heaven, and beheld the souls of martyrs under
the altar, and heard them pray, and he heard it distinctly announced that the answer to their heavenly
prayers depended upon the unfinished work among
their brethren down upon the earth. God's vast family

is one, though part be in heaven and part on earth. In the prayers of Queen Esther we get a glimpse into those mighty pleadings of the saints in heaven, and near the throne, for the other portion of God's people, who, like poor Mordecai, are out wailing in the streets.

10. Next comes the most marvelous deliverance of Mordecai and his people, and the swift and awful doom that overtook Haman. This is all prophetic of the terrific downfall of the Antichrist, who shall be cast alive into the lake of fire. (Compare 2 Thess. 2:8 with Rev. 19:20.) Then the oppressed ones went free with such gladness that the other nations were alarmed and joined in friendly terms with the people of Mordecai, which is a type that when Antichrist is overthrown, the Jewish people will be restored and grafted again upon the sweet olive tree, as Jesus and Paul teach us, and exalted, like the oppressed Mordecai, to the leadership of all the nations, while the glorified saints, and especially those who compose the wife of the Lamb, like the lovely Esther, will shine in dazzling splendor of glory and authority in the palaces of the New Jerusalem. It is all a true story of matchless, divine love; and of the ministry of deepest sorrow, and crucifixion of self, and the outcome of joy and glory in the ages that are to come.

CHAPTER IX.

THE REDEMPTION OF THE BODY.

There is an intimate connection between the experiences of the spiritual life and the clearness and correctness with which scriptural truth is held in the mind. A crooked theology will inevitably produce either fictitious religious experiences, or mystify and cripple a serious one. The subject of the redemption of the body is a problem around which more religious eperiences have gone to wreck than perhaps any other thing. In order to have a scriptural understanding of the redemption of the body, we need to consider the entire scope of redemption as it applies to the three kingdoms of nature, grace and glory. God's blessed dominion is one extending over the whole universe, but for the sake of convenience, and to facilitate our grasp of truth, spiritual writers have divided creation into three kingdoms—nature, grace and glory. So let us notice the redemption accomplished by Jesus as applied to these three kingdoms. The word redemption means to buy back any person or thing which has been captured or forfeited, and inasmuch as the world was captured by Satan, and man forfeited eternal life by sin, Jesus has redeemed or bought back man from sin and the world from Satan's authority. The purchase treasure has been in the life and death of Jesus, but the

(87)

effects of the purchase will be consummated in its ultimate form at the final judgment.

But redemption is being wrought out in its results, first in nature, then in grace, and will issue in that of glorification. St. Paul covers all these thoughts in the 8th chapter of Romans, where he represents all creation, and even the work of grace in our hearts, as waiting for its highest manifestation at the time of the redemption of our bodies.

I. The redemption purchase of Jesus is related to the kingdom of nature. Unless the eternal Son of God had agreed, before the world was made, to his incarnation and death for the human race, then just as soon as Adam sinned, his natural life would have been cut off, all the animals would have perished, and this fair earth would have been shrouded in the blackness of utter desolation. But by virtue of the covenant of redemption the natural kingdom was maintained, the effects of sin were modified and postponed, the animals and natural product of the earth, and the beautiful law of nature were allowed to move on, the human race was permitted to propagate under a system of merciful probation, and thus every rolling sea, every rising and setting sun, every green landscape, every blessing that comes in the natural life of men, animals, or insects, was secured and perpetuated because Jesus agreed to pay for it all by the sacrifice of himself. Thus men have the privilege of living, and thinking, and seeking happiness, and have an opportunity of accepting salvation, and proving whether they will choose righteousness or sin, because the privilege has been bought for them by the Saviour. Every man alive to-day on earth is alive and has the use of his faculties because Jesus died. Hence it is in this sense that the apostle says, "Jesus is the Saviour of all men, but especially of them that believe," that is, Jesus gives all men natural life, with its thousand-fold advantages, and then he becomes in a special way the Saviour from sin of those who receive him into their hearts. This redemption in its relation to the natural life of mankind is unconditional, and life, the universal sunshine, throws its golden mantle alike over the just and the unjust.

II. Redemption in relation to the kingdom of grace. This embraces the whole range of moral and spiritual renovation and restoration to God. It includes the giving of the law, that it may form a standard of right, and also be the minister to search the heart and manifest the nature and extent of sin, for the great office of God's law is not to save but to show us sin and diagnose our disease; but none the less it is God's grace that gives us the law to show us our need of grace. It also includes the work of repentance, justification, sanctification, the fullness of the Spirit, the healing of physical diseases for gracious purposes, divine correction, and the perfect victory of the soul over the devil and the fear of death. These are the great items embraced in the kingdom of grace which could include many subdivisions and many elaborate trains of thought.

Now, one of the greatest mistakes which is made on the subject of divine healing is in not putting it as a part of the kingdom of grace. There are two extreme views which unbalanced or uninstructed minds hold in connection with the healing of bodily diseases by faith. One view is in ignoring divine healing for the body entirely, as having any relation with the gracious redemption of Jesus, and so relegating it to the region of fanaticism or chance. The other extreme view is in putting divine healing as in some way connected with glorification, and as being a part of the redemption of the body from the grave, and thus taking the subject of healing out of the kingdom of grace and making it a part of the kingdom of glory, and this inevitably leads to the rankest fanaticism, and plays sad havoc with the Christian life. Many persons take the words of Paul, in Romans 8:11, where we are told that the Spirit which raised Jesus from the dead will also quicken our mortal bodies, and push them into an extreme application. The direct and main application of that verse is that the Holy Spirit will cause the dead bodies of Christians to be brought to life again and rise from the grave just as truly as the Holy Spirit raised the dead body of Jesus from the tomb. The word "quicken" means to make alive, and the word mortal means dying or subject to death. Now, in a minor sense, this quickening applies to divine healing, simply because the greater includes the less, and if the Holy Spirit, because he has once lived in our bodies, will raise them again from the dust of the grave, how much more can He now, for gracious purposes, heal the diseases of the body by expelling sickness with the virtue of the life of Jesus.

But when persons take divine healing as a part of

glorification, and draw the conclusion that because diseases are healed they can get into a state where their bodies will never die, and then into the delusion that their bodies will be translated even before Christ comes, it leads to wild and unscriptural theories and invariably ruins the person's religious experience, and they become the victims of demons. Some fancy that by long fasting they will lose the principle of death out of their bodies and have physical immortality. Others think that by living a life of celibacy their bodies will become extra holy and so escape death. Some think that by eating only vegetables they will gain physical immortality. Others think if Jesus can heal my body why should he not exempt it entirely from death and the grave? These false notions spring from not understanding that the immortality of the body does not belong at all to the region of probationary grace, but that it lies in the region of glorification, beyond the state of probation and of saving faith.

The thousands of persons that Jesus healed while on the earth were healed as a part of his work of probationary grace, and all of them ultimately died, and he never once hinted about giving immortality except at that day when he would raise the just from the dead. The healing of disease while on probation is included in the kingdom of grace because it relieves suffering and shows forth the compassion of Jesus, and leads people to accept him more fully, and for the purpose of being witnesses for Christ and of using their health in his service.

All these things lie in the region of grace. But as

soon as any one begins to stretch and strain themselves into some awful tension after physical immortality they at once become the victims of evil spirits, who
are always hunting for people on to whom they can
fasten. Healing the body of disease is distinctively a
work of grace, but exempting it from all immortality is
distinctively a work of glory. We must keep these
scriptural distinctions in our minds, or we will go to
wreck both in faith and practice. Hence, divine healing should never strictly be spoken of as the redemption
of the body, which is a Scripture word that refers expressly to raising the dead body from the grave. And
yet we do and may use the word redemption in a general way to include all the economy of grace.

III. Redemption in relation to glorification. The
kingdom of glory includes all the ultimate results of the
redemption wrought by Jesus, such as raising the dead
bodies of believers, or translating and glorifying their
bodies at his second coming; also, the complete rec-
tification of the mental faculties, and the uniting of
body and soul in a form of transcendant glory, like the
glorified Christ, never again to be separated, or to be
sick, or subject to pain, or mistake, or deformity, or
weakness of any kind, but fitted in everything for a
heavenly and divine mode of existence. The work of
glorification is of divine sovereignty, the crowning and
consummating of what Jesus purchased by his death.
Redemption is related to the glorified body in three directions. In the first place it is the avenging of the
believer's body on the devil for all he has done in
bringing sin into the world, and inflicting so much

suffering and death on our bodies. When we are raised
to a blazing and beautiful immortality, Satan will receive his punishment for all the evil he has done to us.
Hence the day of resurrection will be the day of divine revenges for all God's people. In the second
place the redemption of our bodies has a relation to rewards, for it is in our glorified bodies that we are to
receive the ocean streams of divine rewards for our
faith and service while we lived in a state of humiliation and subjection to death. It is in these bodies that
we are now to serve Christ, and we are told we shall be
rewarded according to the deeds done in the body, and
when we receive our glorified bodies it will be in those
bodies that we receive our rewards. When the righteous
die they enter into rest, and their works do follow them,
so their rewards will be poured into the glorified body.
This is the thought that runs through a large part of
the 8th of Romans, especially from verses 18 to 28. In
the third place the redemption of the body is directly
related to the divine glory, because, being fashioned
like the glorified body of Jesus, it will be one of the
most beautiful and transcendent vehicles for the showing forth of the glory of God.

In such a radiant form there will be concentrated
all the divine perfections, and wherever such a body
moves it will be a floating orb of light to illustrate the
glory of God as Creator, Redeemer, Law-giver, Father
Rewarder and King. Such a glorified body will serve
as a miniature history of redemption, and will reveal
the character and purposes of God in all the vast do-
mains of nature, grace and glory. It will be the crown

and summit of the results of the incarnation and
death of Jesus. So we see redemption in its full sweep
covers nature and the natural life unconditionally, and
thus covers the regions of grace on the condition of
faith, and then includes the resurrection and glorification of the body on the conditions of divine sovereignty
and the justice of his rewards.

CHAPTER X.

Thus far in the history of the world, every age or dispensation has come to a close in a similar manner. In the end of each age there is a climax of wickedness on the part of mankind, and a decline or falling away of a majority of those who profess to serve God, calling forth the judgments of God; and on the other hand an intense religious heroism and devotion on the part of the few who have constituted the jewels of God gathered out from the wreckage of that dispensation. Such was the case when God took Abraham and Sarah from the Nimrod age, and such was the case when God gathered the Hebrews from the wreckage of the wicked nations of Egypt and Canaan, and such was the case at the close of the Jewish age when He gathered the little company in the upper room at Pentecost, and such will be the case at the end of this age.

The prophecy of Malachi draws a picture which very accurately fitted in with the close of the Jewish age, and will just as truly fit in with the close of the church age. After describing the terrible condition in the nation, he gives us an account of a little band of holy ones that met frequently for prayer and religious conversation. "Then they that feared the Lord spake often one to another, and the Lord hearkened and heard it; and a book of remembrance was written before Him, for them that feared the Lord, and that thought upon His name. And they shall be mine, saith the Lord of hosts, in that day when I make up my jewels, and I will spare them as a man spareth his own son that serveth him. Then shall ye return, and discern between the righteous and the wicked, between him that serveth God and him that serveth Him not." Mal. 3: 16-18.

These verses present all the features applicable to God's true saints at the winding up of every age; and they are to have their perfect accomplishment at the approaching close of the present Church Age. Let us notice these words in detail.

1. "They that feared the Lord." The word "fear" is the Old Testament term for the expression of godliness and holiness as the word "love" is the more special term used in the New Testament. The Old Testament standard was "walking in the fear of the Lord all the day long," but the New Testament standard is "walking in love as God's dear children." This kind of fear is not the slavish, tormenting fear, which is to be cast out by perfect love, but the basis of reverence and a dread of sin, out of which comes godliness. It is that fear which is "the beginning of wisdom." Fear and love are the two hemispheres to holiness. Fear is the law side, and love is the grace side. Fear by itself would lead to sadness, and love by itself would lead to license. Fear is the root, and love is the tree. Fear runs down into the dark, cool shadows of the earth, and takes firm hold on the rocks of truth, while love runs up in the sunlight, bearing bloom and fruit. Fear gives stam-

ina to the gentleness of love. Fear is the buckram in the white robe of holiness. We really fear those most whom we love most. Thus fear is the Old Testament form of love, and love is the New Testament form of fear.

2. "They spake often one to another." Religious conversation, personal testimony to the inward operations of Divine grace, is the badge of all true piety, and has marked every period of religious revival in the history of the world.

With the death of the class meeting among the Methodists is the death of all their fruitfulness. Verbal testimony to heart felt salvation is a double necessity, for in the first place out of the abundance of the heart the mouth will speak, and in the second place if the testimony is stopped, the grace will leak out of the heart. It is thrilling to read the history of the various revivals through the dark ages, among the Waldenses, the French huguenots, the German reformers, the Scotch covenanters, the early Quakers, and then the Methodists, and now in the modern holiness movement, and trace the same feature among them all, of reaction from formalism, and of personal testimony to the inward work of the Holy Spirit. Just as fire will die without ventilation, so the heat and power of Divine love will die out of the heart without testimony. Malachi distinctly intimates that this religious mark of talking about salvation, and giving personal testimony to it will, in a special way, distinguish the holy ones who will comprise God's jewels in that day when Christ comes. That will be a sad day for the great multitude of church members who have no relish for conversing on holiness, and no testimony to the cleansing blood of the Lamb.

3. "The Lord heard it, and a book of remembrance was written before him." God appreciates being praised and loved, and every testimony to salvation spreads the honor of His Son, and magnifies, and advertises His grace. Hence in all generations He has had His recording angels keep an accurate record of the religious conversations and testimonies of His people. This "book of remembrance" referred to here, is not the same as the Book of Life. The Apostle John shows us the difference between the Book of Life, which simply registers the names of those who are saved, and tells us there were other books out of which the great and the small are to be judged, according to their works (Rev. 20:12). We must distinguish between the simple fact of being saved and the receiving of rewards. Salvation is by faith, but rewards are always according to works. Salvation is received in the present moment, but according to Scripture, no servant of God is ever rewarded till the second coming of Christ. Rev. 22:12.

Salvation is received secretly in the heart, but the reward will be open and visible (Matt. 6:6).

All the saints in heaven will be equally saved from sin, but there will be well-nigh an infinity of variety and degrees of rewards. In order to get a Scripture idea of this book of remembrance, out of which the saints will each receive his appropriate reward, let us notice an incident in the life of Queen Esther. Haman had plotted to kill the Jews, and the saintly old Mordecai and the other Jews had fasted and prayed for deliverance.

The night before, King Ahasuerus could not sleep, and thinking that something had gone wrong in his government, he called for the book of records in which the daily chronicles of the government were kept. On reading this book of remembrance, he found that the humble Mordecai had never been rewarded for delivering the king's life from a plot of murderers, and at once had the good man exalted and rewarded for his fidelity. In a similar way the government of God is conducted according to absolute justice to every creature, both as to rewards and punishments.

There are certain things of a temporal nature which are rewarded or punished in this life, but those things which are spiritual have their rewards or punishments in the age to come. These rewards for God's people will extend down to the infinitesimal things, as our Savior tells us, even to our words, or a cup of cold water. And Malachi says that the book of remembrance is written for those who feared the Lord, and thought upon His name. God's name is His character, including all of His blessed perfections, and every time that one of His servants deliberately fastens his thought upon God in loving meditation, or adoring fear, it is registered in the book of remembrance. In the sight of God a thought is an act, and if His punishments extend down to evil thoughts, so His bright and beautiful rewards are to be bestowed upon every act of mental worship.

Holy fear is in the heart, and worshipful thoughts are in the mind, and these are the two poles of that current of loving fire which marks a life of entire devotion to Jesus. If our thoughts upon God are recognized and

registered by Him as acts of loving worship, and it is so
easy to think of Him, and if we can think of Him under
all circumstances, and in every position of life, why are
we not pouring out around His blessed throne ceaseless
showers of bright, silvery thoughts to gladden His heart,
and repay Him in some little measure, for that eternal
sea of thought which He is constantly pouring over us
even from everlasting.

4. "They shall be mine in that day when I make up
my jewels," or as the margin reads, my "special treasures." The expression "they shall be mine" does not
imply that they are not already the Lord's, but that
when Jesus returns they shall be His by open acceptance
of them, and they shall be blessedly and eternally appropriated as His special property forever. We say the
crown of a kingdom belongs to the heir apparent, but on
the day of coronation the crown becomes his by an au-
gust and public act of appropriation; and so the saints
are to be publicly appropriated as the Lord's possession
in the day of His return. The expression "that day"
refers to the second coming of Christ, called "the day
of the Lord," that is the dispensation of His open manifested glory and kingdom on earth. The expression,
"make up my jewels," refers to the gathering together
the elect saints of all generations, and forming them
into that glorious portable city which St. John says is
the Bride of the Lamb.

Every one who is saved from hell and sin is a treasure
to God, but this word refers to a class whose entire devotion made them "special treasures," or "crown jewels,"
that are to fill the highest rank in the coming kingdom.

The Scriptures abundantly teach that not all of the
saved ones compose the Bride of the Lamb, but that in
every generation there have been those who were entirely
yielded to God, sanctified by His Spirit, who had the
martyr metal in them, and these are to compose the
queenly company who sit by Christ's side in the coming
age, "dressed in the gold of Ophir," who "are to be
princes in all the earth;" and beside this company there
are others spoken of as "honorable women," and as "the
daughter of Tyre," and as "the virgins her companions."
Psalm. 45:9-16.

5. "I will spare them as a man spareth his own son."
What can this mean? It does not refer to sparing them
from hell, for all the saved ones are spared from that
place. It does not mean from death, for millions of holy
ones have died. It must refer to sparing them from
some calamity or form of judgment that not only sinners have but that unfaithful servants pass through. It
would seem clear that it refers to sparing the most devoted saints from the great tribulation judgments, similar to taking in the five wise virgins, and leaving on the
outside the virgins who had no oil and went into the
tribulation. But how can this be applied to all those
who have died? We know not the details, but it is positively affirmed in Scripture, that among all the saved
ones, whether dead or alive, at Christ's coming some will
have advantages, honors and blessings, that others do
not have. The apostle speaks of those who will be saved,
and yet says, "they shall suffer loss." 1 Cor. 3:12-15.
Thus the jewel saints are spared from these losses, and if
living, spared from the great tribulation.

6. "Then shall ye return." This indicates clearly that the real saints of the Lord are first gathered out from the earth, and taken away from that awful period of tribulation, which Jesus says is to exceed anything the world has ever known, and then afterward are to return back to the earth with their Master.

There is no way possible to understand the reading of this Scripture, except in the light of the pre-millennial coming of Jesus.

7. "Ye shall discern between the righteous and the wicked." That is, after the saints, who have been spared from the tribulation judgments, return with their Lord back to the earth, they having been glorified, will be endowed with all spiritual gifts, including judicial authority, to have power over the nations. The word discern" implies perfect spiritual vision, to read the secrets of men's souls as quickly and easily as you discern colors in a landscape. The New Testament words to "judge" and to "discern" are the same words in the Greek. Hence this passage from Malachi positively affirms that the crown jewel saints are to *"return"* back to this earth with spiritual gifts and power to discern and judge all the nations that survive the tribulation period, and these high honors of "judging the world," as Paul says, will be a part of those magnificent rewards for having feared the name, and having frequently "spoken one to another" about God, and for all their good deeds which were recorded in the book of remembrance.

CHAPTER XI.

CHRIST CALLING HIS BRIDE.

"The voice of my beloved; behold he cometh leaping upon the mountains; skipping upon the hills." "My beloved spake and said unto me, Rise up, my love, my fair one, and come away." The Song of Solomon will never be understood in its completeness until Jesus comes, and gathers His elect saints to the marriage supper of the lamb. In the second chapter of the Songs of Solomon, we have a prophetic vision of Christ's second coming and gathering out His bridehood saints unto Himself. Let us notice in detail the various points in the vision.

1. The voice of the Bridegroom. The power and sweetness of this voice is referred to many times in Scripture. "Let me hear thy voice; for sweet is thy voice, and thy countenance is beautiful." "My sheep hear my voice, and I know them and they follow me." John the Baptist said that he was the friend of the Bridegroom, and rejoiced when he heard the Bridegroom's voice. The Apostle John heard the voice of Jesus in the Isle of Patmos, and said it was like the sound of many waters.

Jesus, referring to the omnipotent penetration of His voice, says that "the dead which are in their graves

(103)

shall hear His voice, and come forth." We are told that Adam heard that voice walking in the garden of Eden.

Jesus is emphatically the voice of the Father; the eternal outspoken Word from the inner bosom of the Father. The voice of Christ to the soul includes all methods by which He awakens, and wins, and woos, and communicates His will, His knowledge, His fellowship to the obedient believer. He may speak to the soul by a thought, or a vision, or a spiritual sensation, or a spiritual articulation of His word to the inner senses; but whatever form the voice may assume, it penetrates to the depth of the inner spirit, and is recognized as something above the earthly, and the human, and as a divine communication whose power and authenticity is never questioned by the loving, trusting heart.

In every generation, those servants of God who have been entirely yielded to Him, have distinctly recognized the Bride-groom's voice in the depth of their souls. And in every generation, those who have been called into the bridehood of Christ, have had sweet words of such divine relationship spoken in their heart, and have had great premonitions of Christ's return to this earth, and of unutterable joys and honors which will then be conferred upon those who in this life have entered into a real living union with God.

2. Christ's special manifestations to His bride. "Behold He standeth behind our wall; He looketh forth at the windows, showing Himself through the lattice."

If we group together several expressions in this Song of Solomon, we get a picture like the following:

King David has a palace on a high hill overlooking the
surrounding country. Beyond the city wall the king
has a large vineyard, in which many men and maidens
are working. Among the maidens working in the vineyard, and getting sun-burnt, is the humble, beautiful
daughter of an honorable Jewish family, whose sisters
taunt her for doing such humble labor, and gettting
sun-burnt and neglecting her own selfish interests at
home. But the prince, Solomon, is in love with her, and
when he walks on the veranda of his father's palace, he
signals to her through the window lattice, and, as the
margin indicates, flourishes his hand in love tokens,
which she perceives and sweetly responds to, while at
work in his father's vineyard. This explains all those
expressions when the bride says, "they made me the
keeper of the vineyards, but mine own vineyard—my
selfish interests—have I not kept." "I am sun-burnt—
for the word "black" would be translated "sun-burnt"
—but beautiful, O ye daughters of Jerusalem." "Frown
not upon me" (the word "look" signifies to frown, or to
look with a scowl). She says to her proud sisters who
scowl upon her, because she works in the vineyard and
bemeans herself with such humble service: "frown not
upon me because I am sunburnt, because the sun hath
frowned upon me; my mother's children were angry
with me." How true it always is that unsanctified church
members, who cultivate their own selfish vineyards, look
with angry scowls upon the humble sanctified ones, who
go forth beyond the city walls, and sectarian fences, to
bear the heat and burden of the day, and endure the
sun-scorching of persecution, ostracism, and various

trials, which timid and selfish Christians are not willing to bear.

But the King's son, the Divine Solomon, from his
Father's palace on high, looks out upon the humble sun-
burnt saints at work in His Father's vineyard, to whom
He is secretly espoused, and through the lattice of the
skies manifests Himself to them in such vivid tokens of
love, as to cause them a joy, notwithstanding their
trials, far surpassing the comforts of other professed
Christians, who are not utterly abandoned to a love-
service for the glory of their Lord.

3. The translation of the bride. "My beloved
spake, and said unto me, Rise up my love, my fair one,
and come away." As the bride must first know the voice
of her beloved, and then the private personal manifestation of his love, so in the next place there comes the
time when he calls the bride to depart from her old
home, and go with him to his own mansion. All these
steps are carried out, both in Christ's dealing with the
individual soul espoused to Him, and also in that great
body of elect saints that constitute the perfected bride
of the Lamb. And so these words are to be fulfilled
when Christ comes in the air, and with His omnipotent
voice calls the bodies of His dead saints to rise up from
their graves, and calls the living wise virgins who have
the oil of the Holy Spirit in their hearts, to rise up
from the earth, and go away with the Bridegroom into
that mansion of pure gold which He has built for them.
When Jesus returned to Bethany, after His absence
across the Jordan, He called for both the living and
the dead; for Martha said to Mary, "Arise, for the Mas-

ter is come, and calleth for thee"; and then in a few moments, He called unto Lazarus to arise and come forth from the grave.

This incident is prophetic of the time when He returns from His long absence, and will again speak to the living saints like Mary, and the dead saints like Lazarus, the words of our text, "Rise up my love, my fair one, and come away."

4. The Summer Age. "For lo, the winter is past, the rain is over and gone, and the flowers appear on the earth."

The long domination of Satan and sin, the protracted generations of corrupt human governments, with war, and whiskey, and oppression, and with all their attendant sorrows, constitutes the long winter of human history; but when Christ returns to reign on earth with His glorified saints, this long winter of wickedness will come to its close, and the reign of righteousness will bring the glorious summer to the nations of the earth. This Scripture, like hundreds of others, is to have a double fulfillment; first in the individual believer, and then in the world at large. Thus, when the believer is purified through the blood of Jesus, and the Comforter comes to abide, the spiritual winter, with the cold, wet rains of anguish and moral misery terminates; and the summer of pure love spreads itself abroad in the heart and life. But this is only a preliminary fulfillment of these precious words, for the great world is like a giant individual, and Satan is to the world what the carnal mind is to the soul, and when Satan is dethroned from the world, and chained in the abyss, and Jesus sets up His theocratic kingdom on earth, the summer of millennial glory will fill the world as the waters fill the sea. Christ often compares His second coming to the coming of summer.   Luke 21:27-31.

5. The singing age. "The time for the singing of *birds is come.*" The word "birds" is in italics, which indicates that it is not in the original Hebrew Scripture, and the passage would be much better rendered "the singing age has come." In this age, as well as all past ages, there is pre-eminently the fact of weeping and sorrow, and even the best saints of God find the words of Christ true that in the present world (or age) they should have tribulation. Human history in the present age is marked with sickness, pain and death.

Not only the wicked, but the wisest and holiest of men, must endure poverty, disappointment, temptation, sore trials, loneliness, persecution, and at the very best condition of things in the present age, there is much inevitable suffering and weeping. But there is a better age coming, and God's enemies on earth are to become a footstool for the peaceful steps of the King of eternal love, and there is to come an age of singing and world-wide gladness, in which universal joy and music will reign pre-eminent. The Scriptures abound with prophecies of that day. "For ye shall go out with joy, and be led forth with peace; the mountains and the hills shall break forth before you into singing, and all the trees of the field shall clap their hands." It is well to note that these words are spoken in connection with the promise that Christ as David shall be a leader of the nations on the earth. See Isa. 55:3-12.

The Apostle Paul refers to this singing age in the eighth of Romans, when he contrasts the "groaning of creation" in the present age, to that blessed period when this groaning creation "shall be delivered from its present bondage, into the glorious liberty of the children of God." A great many of the Psalms prophesy an age of universal singing. "Make a joyful noise unto the Lord all the earth; sing unto the Lord with the harp, with trumpets and cornets; let the hills be joyful together before the Lord, for He cometh to judge the earth; with righteousness shall He judge the world." Psalm 98. Please notice that this world-wide singing is distinctly mentioned as a consequence of the coming of the Lord to judge and govern the world. The bridehood saints that are translated or resurrected, after being received by the Bridegroom in the air, are to come back with Him, and through their dominion, under Christ, over the nations on earth, the whole world will be filled with anthems of praise, which is referred to about fifty times in the prophecies on that subject.

6. The world-wide fullness of the Holy Spirit. This is referred to by the expression "the voice of the turtle is heard in your land." The word "turtle" in this verse refers to the dove, and the dove is a synonym of the Holy Spirit. Hence, in the coming age, when the heavenly Bridegroom and His bridehood saints shall reign on the earth, the voice of the Holy Spirit will be heard everywhere in the land; and instead of a few feeble revivals, such as we have in the present age, where only a few scores, or at least a few hundreds, are regenerated against fearful odds of difficulty, then the Holy Spirit

will inundate the world, and millions to be saved in those great millennial revivals, when a nation shall be born in a day. The words of Joel about the Spirit being poured out upon all flesh will then be fulfilled more perfectly than ever in the past.

Every successive age has been characterized by a great increase of the operations of the Holy Spirit. In the age before the flood, He strove with men, with very few results of saving power. In the Jewish age the Spirit was manifest in more than ten-fold degree over the ante-diluvian age; and in the Christian age the Holy Spirit has been given in a thousand-fold greater measure than in the Jewish age; and on the same ratio, in the coming millennial age, the Spirit will be poured out on the nations in all the earth a million-fold more than in the present age, so that it will be emphatically true, the dove-like voice of the Holy Spirit will be heard in all the earth.

CHAPTER XII.

In all the history of spiritual literature, one subject of the greatest importance is that of Divine recollection. As many who read this may not have had facilities for extensive religious reading, it may be well to give a sort of definition of what Divine recollection is. To be recollected refers to a state where the mind is calm, and all the faculties are collected with such attentiveness to our surroundings, or relation with God, our adjustment to providence, and the work we have in hand, as to be consciously awake and observant in all these directions. It is called Divine recollection, because the mental faculties are collected in God, in a state of mental prayer. The following points may help us to a clearer view of the subject:

First. Divine recollection is to pay a double attention to God and ourselves. It is to keep the mind stayed on the Lord, His universal presence and providence, and at the same time to keep an eye upon our position before God, to watch the dispositions or thoughts that spring up within us, and to carefully remember the duties we have in hand, and to constantly associate ourselves and our work with God. It is similar to the attention which a locomotive engineer gives to his engine and to the track, keeping his hand on the throttle, and his eye upon

the iron rails ahead. It is a task which requires firm
nerves, and close mental application, for the mind must
keep up a double action through the hand in one direc-
tion, and through the eye in another. This same double
action of attractiveness is also exhibited in the helmsman
on a ship, who must have his thoughts constantly collected upon the compass, the wheel, and the open sea that
stretches away before him. To think of God, without
constant reference to our conduct and character, would
produce only cold, speculative philosophy about him;
on the other hand, to think only of ourselves, without
constantly yielding ourselves up to the will of God,
would produce self-righteous Phariseeism. But this
double action of calm, deliberate recollection of God
and ourselves, constantly enthrones Him in our lives,
and constantly blends all our movements with His
grace and providence.

Second. There is a necessity of all Christians who
advance in holiness, of forming this habit of Divine
recollection, or no headway can be made in the things
of God. When the soul is first converted, or first sanctified, there is a freshet of celestial rain, which accom-
plishes wonders for the soul, and seems to carry us by
a heavenly momentum a good ways on our journey, without any special effort on our part; and multitudes of
Christians expect the great showers that inundate the
soul at such times, to nearly relieve them of any deliberate effort to use their mental powers in acquiring the
knowledge of God.

In a very wet season farmers cannot plow, and the
rain seems to monopolize the work, but when the water

has run off the ground, unless they diligently get to work with their plows, the ground will bake hard and strangle the crop. There is something just like this in the spiritual life. When the freshets of grace are pouring down on the soul, they seem to supercede any necessity for spiritual reading, or plodding perseverance, or habits of deliberate recollection, or patient interior mental prayer. But when these sweet floods have run their legitimate course, unless the soul applies itself to a life of diligence in plowing the soil, and training the vines, and bringing the mental powers under the discipline of Divine recollection, the soil of the heart will soon pack hard, the mind run to weeds, and the tongue run away with loquacity, and the very floods of grace will yield no fruit. Divine recollection is like keeping the mind in a heavenly climate, where all the graces can grow and ripen to perfection. Constant recollections in God, is that even temperature of the soul, in which it can render the best service, perform the greatest works of righteousness, and at the same time put into these works the most solid devotion to God. Salvation starts in the emotions, but if it does not take hold on the mental powers, and fasten itself into persistent efforts of spiritual thinking, and reading, and praying, it will inevitably pass away like the evaporation of morning dew. Here is where thousands who were once shouting happy in the Lord have failed, and are now twice dead, because they never, from the depths of their nature, determined to make Christ-likeness the business of their lives. They would be saints, providing they could float down the river all the time on a raft in a revival freshet. Only a few

Christian people put their brains in the service of God. They may believe in loving God with all their hearts, but not with all their minds, and all their will power.

Third. The blessed habit of Divine recollection must be acquired by degrees, and is not to be misunderstood with the instantaneous cleansing. Still, some persons acquire it a great deal more rapidly than others, and great trouble, or mortification of spirit, wonderfully facilitates a soul in acquiring deep recollectedness of God; for whatever most thoroughly tears us away from the world, or knocks the earthly props away from under us, or detaches us from all creatures, and drives us most profoundly into the bosom of God, will serve to spiritualize the mind, and assist in forming habits of constant mental prayer. There is no easy, royal road to the practice of Divine recollection; it must be acquired with effort, yet not with any over straining or vehemence of spirit, for any effort of the soul that chafes or discourages, or produces turbulence, is not of grace. One of the steps in the acquisition of Divine recollection is that of silence, or checking ourselves when we are about to speak, and mentally asking ourselves, is there a real need for us to speak, and what good will it do, and is our speaking a mere impulse of self. Millions of words would never be uttered, if professing Christians, if even the professors of holiness, would practice this mortification of silence. The crucifixion of the tongue to so much talk comes after the crucifixion of inbred sin in the heart, and is accomplished by very few. Another step to holy recollection is to check all eagerness for the hearing of news, and wanting to know everything about

the foolish world around. Sinners and baby Christians
pride themselves on keeping up with the times, which
simply means, without their knowing it, they are keeping in with Satan's procession.

Newspapers keep multitudes from a life of prayer,
and the interior knowledge of themselves, and communion with God. The news we ought to know can very
quickly be learned.

Another step to recollection, is to avoid any effort
to make a show of our religion, to study simplicity,
never to make an ostentation of holiness, but to live as
holy as possible without ever wanting to show it off.
Nothing would be a greater crucifixion to some Christians than to refrain themselves from ever making a display of their religion.

Hence, in the practice of silence, or the speaking of
few words when in company, we should never do it in
such a way as to render ourselves singular, ill-mannered,
but with modesty and sweetness of spirit.

Another method of recollection, is not to over-burden
ourselves with work or manifold cares. Nature likes to
bustle, and rush, and do many things, but grace is just
the opposite.

Fourth. It is in a state of Divine recollection that
we can catch the inspirations of the Holy Ghost, and detect the guiding hand of our heavenly Father's providence. It is the only condition of clear spiritual vision,
where the soul can detect the approaches of temptation,
and the devices of Satan, which always have a look of
reason, or beauty, or winsome successfulness, or philan-
thropic air about them. The Devil paints all his plans

with something plausible, and it requires a spiritual eye that is clear, and steady, and slow, to look through the point, and discover the fraud. And finally it is only in a state of Divine recollection that we keep in a frame of mental prayer. When the soul has a holy recollectedness, it can at any time engage in prayer, with some depth and fervor of heart.

For lack of recollection, when many Christians go to prayer, it takes all their time to get disengaged from the rush and noise of life, and to empty out the perplexities from their hearts, and the images from their minds, and when the season of prayer is ended, they have scarcely reached the starting place of real prayer to their heavenly Father. It is holy recollection in the soul that gives solidity and weight to Christian life, it shuts off wildness, foolishness, levity, talkativeness, it keeps the mental faculties elevated, well balanced, and in an attitude to meet Jesus. This habit of Divine recollection is precisely what the apostle means, "by girding up the loins of our mind, and being sober, and hoping to the end, for the grace we shall receive at the revelation of Jesus Christ."

CHAPTER XIII.

THE JOYS OF HEAVEN.

When some poor family in the old world contemplates emigrating to that new and wonderful country in the West for the betterment of all their circumstances with what thrilling interest they gather all the information they can about the new world. They eagerly devour books and maps describing the country, its mountains and prairies, its rivers and mines, its climate and productiveness, and methods of travel, as to how to get there, and what the cost will be. All these characteristics will mark the conduct of those souls that are true emmigrants from earth to heaven. From the days of Abraham till now, the life of a true servant of God has been that of a pilgrim. The learned and saintly Dean Alford had inscribed upon his tomb, "The lodge of a pilgrim on his way to the New Jerusalem." Both a prophet and an apostle unite in telling us that the joys of the heavenly kingdom are greater than the heart of man can comprehend. Ever since Abraham got a vision of the city which hath foundations, and was so charmed with the prospect of the sweet immortal joys in that city, that he never would build himself a house, but lived in tents, the saints of all generations have looked forward to the supreme happiness of that heavenly country; and hoped, and sung and meditated, and sweetly longed to reach its ever-blessed enjoyments. There are three vast empires in the universal creation, recognized in Scripture as Nature, Grace and Glory. We first live in a state of nature, and learn much of its character, its laws, its beauties, its pleasures, and also of its fallen condition, its vanity and transitoriness. When we become real Christians we enter, by the new birth, into the realm of grace. The system of grace is a distinct economy in the creation of God for the saving of a fallen world, involving a plan of redemption by the incarnation and sacrificial death of the second Person in the Godhead, and a life of faith, until our probation ends. This realm of grace has its joys, and victories, though mingled in manifold ways with the ministry of sorrow, and of sore temptations and trials. Beyond the realm of grace comes the realm of glory, with its unmeasured vastness of liberty and honor, of happiness and unfading immortality. It is upon this realm of heavenly glory that we want to fix our eyes for a few moments, that by looking at the future glory we may strengthen the present conditions of grace.

Perhaps we ought first of all to form some scriptural idea of what is meant by the word "heaven." This word as used in the Bible, is a large, generic term, including all the sinless creation of God outside of this world, and outside of the hell, which we are told was specially prepared for the devil and his angels. The Hebrew word for heaven is in the plural, and literally means "things heaved up"; that is, all things elevated above this world. The Greek word for heaven is frequently in the plural number, and includes all things above the earth. The

word signifies things in the air and in the sky. In scores
of places the term heaven includes our atmosphere, and
cloud regions, which is the first heaven. It next includes the sky, with its sun, moon and stars, which is
the second heaven. Beyond that is the third heaven,
to which Paul was caught up, including the unknown
localities of Paradise, the abode of departed saints, and
the throne of God, the divine court, where countless angels minister and worship. Now, when we speak of the
joys of heaven that are in reserve for the righteous, we
must widen our thought, according to the extent of
Scripture teaching, to embrace all that belongs to the
glorified and immortal state. We must also remember
that when this world has passed through its history of
redemption, and when its various dispensations of grace
have been merged into the age of glory, it will be in
the boundaries of heaven, and a part of that blessed
realm; hence, we now use the word heaven more especially to apply to the glorified state of the saints, including the resurrection of the body, the marriage supper of
the Lamb, the princely authority over the nations with
Jesus in His millennial reign, and the beatific vision of
seeing the face of God, and the glorious ministries and
immortal honors that are to come after the institution of
the new heavens and the new earth, and the domesti-
cating of the glorified saints in their mansions in the
city of pure gold, the New Jerusalem.

1. *The Glorified Body.* All our best thoughts
in connection with the joys of possessing a glorified body
must be formed out of faint analogies and consist mostly
of negatives, as it will be in so many things the very

opposite of what the body is in the present state. The bodies of the resurrected saints will be of the same substance they are now; in fact the same bodies, according to Scripture; but the particles composing the body will be transmuted from fleshly conditions into a spiritualized condition, from the mortal to the immortal; from being subject to physical law, they will be under spiritual law, having passed from the realm of nature into the realm of glory. The Apostle says of the resurrected body of the saint, "that it is sown in corruption, it is raised in incorruption; it is sown in dishonor, it is raised in glory; it is sown in weakness, it is raised in power; it is sown a natural body, it is raised a spiritual body." 1 Cor. 15:42-44. These four attributes of the glorified body cover the entire range of all the possibilties that we can imagine as belonging to an organism for its everlasting blessedness. The first attribute is that of immortality, perfect exemption from sickness, death, pain, old age, deformity, and every taint of decay. The second attribute is that of glory, which implies its brightness, as of light, also its beauty and radiance and sweet attractiveness, possessing every charm of form and motion, and every capacity for the most brilliant expression of thought and feeling. The third attribute is that of power, angelic energy, which includes supernatural strength over all the forces of nature, such as wind, water, fire, gravitation, storms, lightning, and every known force in the realm of matter. It also includes swiftness of motion, power to fly through space with the ease and velocity of light; as Jesus, after He rose from the dead, could instantly take His body through stone walls without opening a door, or transfer it from the earth to the third heavens and back again in a few moments, and make it visible to men, and then vanish out of their sight at will. This word "power" also includes the vast and transcendent exercise of the five senses, of the voice, of the expression, of the features, so that the power of the glorified body of a saint will surpass any known power in all the realms of nature —power surpassing lightning, thunder, cyclones, earthquakes, rolling oceans, blazing suns, or shooting stars, or all the combined energies of the armies of earth, or of the combined strength of all wicked men and evil angels. When the armies of Assyria besieged Hezekiah, God sent an angel one night, who, with the brush of his wing, swept the breath out of one hundred and eighty five thousand soldiers, and Jesus tells us that the power of a glorified saint shall be equal to that of the angels. The fourth attribute is that of being "spiritual," which includes its spotless purity, its being subtle like a flame, or a body of solidified light, with spiritual senses, ecstacies and joys entirely under the sway of spiritual laws, and of such marvelous capacity as to be flooded with divine bliss without being shattered by the torrents of heavenly gladness. Think of all the joys that the five senses can take in while we are in a state of nature; how the eye can sweep landscapes of surpassing beauty, and ocean and mountain scenery of inspiring grandeur, and how the ear can be thrilled with inspiring or subduing strains of music, or the melody of magnificent poetry, and how the senses can drink in sweet odors and delicious tastes, and the manifold pleasures of feeling which

cover the body at every pore, and yet, all we know of
these material pleasures form but a hint of those exult-
ant joys of the glorified senses in an immortal body.
Perhaps there will be senses belonging to our glorified
bodies which we do not now possess, and of which we
have no conception. Our glorified senses will possess a
range of action, and a quickness and delicacy of power,
which we cannot now imagine. The eye in our glorified
bodies will be both telescopic and microscopic, so that
we can see all objects millions and billions of miles away
without having to use a telescope, and then we can see
the infinitesimal atoms of all things at a glance, without
having to use a microscope as we do now. What must
the joys of vision be, which can sweep out in one tranquil gaze over the multiplied splendor of millions of
worlds, and at the same time delight itself in piercing
through the perfections of God that lie hid away in
every dew drop and every grain of sand! At present our
ears are capable of receiving only a small range of
sounds, and if a sound rises too high, we fail to hear it;
or if it sinks below a certain pitch, we fail to hear it.
There are thousands of sounds constantly vibrating
through the earth and air, which are either too loud
or too low for the capacity of our ears. Now think of
the joys of sound in the boundless sweep of celestial
music, which a glorified ear can receive. It would seem
that the joys of the glorified bodies of the saints would
alone constitute a whole heaven of bliss.

2. *The Glorified Mind.* The heavenly joys of a
glorified intellect will transcend even those of the glorified physical senses. In contrast with the intellectual

pleasures that we now have, our understandings will
drink in unlimited seas of heavenly truth and beauty,
perfectly free from all error or heresy, from all mistake,
blunder or confusion of any kind whatever. On account
of the imperfections in all earthly knowledge, we have
to be re-learning, changing our views, correcting our
measurements, and the joys of knowledge are crippled
by uncertainty. But when our intellects see all things
in their true light, and their beautiful harmony, and
their correct relations with cloudless certainty, and with
an unbroken tranquility of vision behold the secrets of
creation, of science, and philosophy, perfectly free from
all mist, and then have the mental capacity for embrac-
ing in one vast system all the works of God in their various departments, and of seeing how the whole hangs sus-
pended, like a beautiful dream, in the will of God, it
will be an overflowing bliss to our understandings, beyond anything we now know of the thrill of poetry, or
the gladness of some new discovery. Then think of the
expansion of our mental faculties in the glorified state,
with the disclosure, it may be, of many new faculties for
which we have no use in our earthly state, and these
mental faculties so adapted to angels, and saints, and all
created things, as to instantaneously read them, inter-
pret them, understand them, and then to possess all
this knowledge with a calm and perfect self-conscious-
ness, without ever being burdened, or distracted, or over-
excited by such worlds of intellectual truth and grandeur! To have minds forever delivered from all preju-
dice, from all theological or geographical bias, from all
sluggishness and monotony, and so invigorated as to for-

ever expatiate in God, with constant freshness and elasticity of action, and to keep poised in the highest flights of universal knowledge, will certainly constitute one of the great joys of the heavenly state. Just imagine all the intellectual pleasures that belong to this fallen world, the joys of discovering new continents and islands, new stars, new substances in nature, new inventions, the joys of artists in painting pictures, in carving statues, in writing music, in writing poems, the joys of the composition of architects, of orators, of singers, and of scientists, and then take every sort of intellectual pleasure of the race, and lift it into the glorified state, and free it from all sorrow, or sin, from all disappointment, error or imperfection, and stamp on it the fixed radiance of everlasting glory, and you have a faint image of the joys in reserve for the intellects of the saints in heaven.

3. *The Glorified Affections.* The heart is the supreme organ of gladness, and many instances have occurred in which animals and human beings have dropped dead from the sudden access of insupportable joy. What will all the joys of glorified senses and intellects be in comparison with the sweetness and the magnificence of celestial love. Sin has devastated the affections of the human heart more terribly than it has the human intellect, or the five senses. Hence, when we descant on the pleasures of the understanding, or of the bodily senses, the children of men can more readily understand what we are talking about. But when we come to that deeper world of the heart-nature, where sin has wrought its worst effects, it is more difficult for the people of this

world to understand the powerful operation of pure, unselfish, heavenly love. Notwithstanding the havoc sin has made with the human heart, human love is still the strongest of all the forces in the human race, and out of this human love comes the larger portion of all earthly happiness, though it is often in a thousand ways intermingled with sorrow, yet even sorrow in most instances is a form of pathetic love—love under bruises, or love in tears. The joys of heavenly love will be immeasurably beyond the joys of our mere natural affections in this present life.

In order to form a proper conception of what our love will be in the heavenly state, we must put together a few Bible facts. There are two distinct kinds of love mentioned in the Greek Testament—one is *philos,* which includes all the natural affections that men have by creation; and the other is *agape,* which includes the pure love in the divine nature, and such love as fills heaven and the angels. Now we know there are great joys in natural love, even before people are regenerated and brought into saving grace. When souls are saved and living in Christ, they not only have their natural affection, but they have that natural love brought up from nature into grace, and in addition to this, they have the love of God, which is entirely above nature, shed abroad in them by the Holy Spirit. Now, in the heavenly state, our natural love will not be annihilated, because it belongs to us as a part of our creation, the same as our five senses, or our intellects, but this natural affection will be glorified and flooded to the uttermost with the hot ocean of Divine love and the two kinds of love will be forever blended in an ineffable union, as that soul and body are united, even as Christ's divinity and humanity are united. The joys of heavenly love will consist in the following things: It will be a love that is perfectly spotless, utterly free from selfishness, or self-seeking, or danger from the flesh, or from any taint of ill-feeling, or stain of earthliness. It will be a love forever fixed in holiness, without variation, or ebb-tide, or coldness, but an unchanging sweetness of character like the blue color in the sky, or the saltness in the sea, an everlasting warmth of heart like the nature of God. It will be a universal love, overflowing all creation—God, angels and saints—and running down in constant waves of sweetest benevolence to all the lower orders of creation. It will be a most conscious and intelligent love, and not a latent, quiescent principle in the heart, but a wide-awake, all-glowing, all-melting, all-embracing, conscious love, most keenly felt, like a seraphic furnace in every glorified bosom. It will be an all-controlling love, possessing the intellect and the body and filling all the mental faculties, and all the glorified senses, in such a rapturous and all-embracing power, that every part of soul and body will do its bidding. Here is a passage from the saintly Faber, on the bliss of heavenly love: "Oh, to turn our whole souls upon God, and souls thus expanded and thus glorified, to have our affections multiplied and magnified a thousandfold, and then girded up and strengthened by immortality to bear the beauty of God, to be unveiled before us and when strengthened, to be rapt by it into a sublime amazement which has no similitude on earth, to be carried away by the inebriating torrents of love, and yet be firm in the most steadfast adoration; to have passionate desire, yet without tumult or disturbance; to have the most bewildering intensity along with an unearthly calmness; to lose ourselves in God, and then find ourselves the more our own than ever; to love rapturously, and to be loved again still more rapturously; and then for our love to grow more rapturous still, and again the return of our love to be still outstripping what we gave, and still the great transparent waters of God's love to flow over us and overwhelm us, until the vehemence of our peace and adoration and joy reach beyond our most venturesome imagination; what is all this, but for our souls to live a life of the most intelligent ecstacy of love, and yet not to be shivered by the fiery heat."

4. *Glorified Society.* Paul speaks of the riches that God has "in His inheritance in the saints." A human soul redeemed and sanctified by the precious blood of God's own dear Son, and filled with the graces of the Holy Spirit, is a treasure far more precious to our heavenly Father, than all the splendor and material wealth in millions of worlds. On account of our multiplied infirmities in our earthly state, we fail to see or appreciate or enjoy the fulness of the fellowship of those who compose the mystical body of Christ. One of the sorrows that comes to a humble and tender heart in this life is the clash of religious souls, the misunderstandings and the strife between those who really love Jesus, and the scarcity of broad-hearted and intelligent charity and fellowship. "We shall know each other better when the mists have cleared away." One of the great joys

that await us in the heavenly kingdom is that of the most entrancing love and mutual appreciation, with the glorified society of angels and saints. The reciprocal joys in the society of heaven can be faintly imagined from the following considerations: We shall have a perfect and instantaneous recognition of every individual saint, and probably every angel, of all the countless millions in the kingdom of heaven. Scripture tells us that "we shall know even as also we are known," and again, "that we shall see eye to eye when the Lord brings again Zion." The apostles at the transfiguration recognized Moses and Elijah, whom they had never seen. In our present state, most of our knowledge is acquired by the slow process of learning, but in the glorified state knowledge will come through the organ of intuition and by quick flashes of supernatural revelation. Hence the very moment we meet the blessed ones in heaven, we will know by spiritual instinct just who they are, their name, their personality, the great traits that make up their special character, and also know their rank in the heavenly kingdom. What a joy will such recognition contain!

Another form of this joy will be in the mutual, whole-hearted appreciation of each other's character and history, and of the variety of graces and gifts. In the Bible, God compares the righteous to various kinds of trees of the Lord's planting, such as the cedar, the box, the myrtle, the oak, the vine, the palm tree, the olive, and the orange, each of which has a special growth and beauty, a special perfume, ornament and utility. The saints are also compared to various precious stones, as the diamond, the emerald, the ruby, the amethyst, and others that make up the twelve distinct kinds of gems— "the living stones" that go into the structure of the New Jerusalem. No imagination we now have can calculate the delicate and multiplied joys we shall have in heaven, flowing out from the appreciation of all the varieties of the saints of all ages. Those whose gifts and traits of character, of calling and life work, were so unlike and seemingly so opposite while on earth, will in heaven be perfectly understood, appreciated and mutually loved and honored with a most intelligent and generous appreciation. To mingle in those radiant throngs will be like walking through a divine flower garden, where there is an infinite variety of flowers, each adorned with separate beauty and decked in a shade of singular color, and emitting a peculiar perfume belonging only to itself, and each one essential to the perfection of the entire garden.

Many of the things for which God-loving souls are now hated, ostracised, criticised, and misunderstood, will then blossom forth in such light and grace and fragrance, as to make them more appreciated and more tenderly loved. In many ways, the bruises of earth will make the perfumes of heaven. Again, our joy in glorified society will be intensified by a personal love for each and every one in the kingdom of heaven. Our affections will not be blind and indiscriminate, but so strengthened and expanded in divine love, that, like God, there will be in us a particular form of love for every separate angel and saint. In addition to all this, there will be special circles of heavenly friendship, in which the count-

less throngs of the redeemed will be in various ranks
and companies. Paul says that in the resurrection the
saints shall be like the stars, and that "one star differs
from another star in glory." The stars go in families
and circles and various magnitudes. There will be thousands of ranks and degrees of reward, of honor and capacity in heaven. Jesus, when on earth, had His special
friends, and an inner circle with whom He had naturally
more private and personal fellowship. Jesus had a perfect human nature, and in accordance therewith He had
His private and personal friendships, the same as angels
and saints; and this, instead of being a hindrance in
any way to His virtues and graces, was an essential part
of the very perfection of His humanity. The bliss of
the heavenly state will be heightened from the fact that
there will be circles and families and bands and different ranks of angels and saints, who are specially kindred
spirits, with similar gifts and tastes and ministries. This
is beautifully set forth by the different gates and various
foundations and the diversified precious stones that
make up the New Jerusalem. Each glorified soul will
find endless joy in this heavenly variety, and yet a more
private and hidden joy in its own circle of kindred
spirits.

Another feature of glorified social joy will be the
utterly unselfish delight we will have in the happiness of
others. The purest joy that we can have on earth is that
of making others happy, and the gladness we have in
seeing them so. A mother enjoys the happiness of her
little children, and to see them glad is a greater joy to
her than to the children themselves. That eminent

eaint, Alfred Cookman, in one of his letters, gives an account of visiting the Christian home of a young married couple and tells us that as he saw their happiness with each other in their new home, he felt a most exquisite delight spring up in his heart, to see their joys, and that he felt as if the pure gladness of their young hearts in a transcendent way had become his own happiness. This will constitute one of the joys of heaven, that we will feel an unutterable galdness in seeing others rewarded, and in the beauty of their crowns, and the honor of their various ranks, and in the richness of their multiplied gifts, and thus our joy in the blessedness of others will be multiplied as many times as there are happy spirits in the countless hosts of our Father's kingdom.

5. *The Joys of Glorified Service.* The activities of the glorified state, the lofty responsibilities with which we shall be invested, the thrones of authority to which we may be appointed, the delicate and solemn stewardship entrusted to our hands, the exercise of all our faculties in carrying out the plans of our heavenly Father, the songs we shall sing, the entrancing music that our fingers will sweep from golden harps, the melodious hallelujahs of praise that our immortal voices will pour forth, with the diapason thunder roll of the organ of eternity, will form one of the mighty streams of heavenly joy.

The story is told of a company of monks, debating among themselves as to what would be the greatest joy in heaven, and several having given their opinion, they asked the quiet old Thomas a'Kempis his opinion, and he pointed to that verse in Revelation, "His servants shall serve Him." Nowhere in the Bible is it represented that the spirits of departed saints in Paradise are engaged in active service while their bodies sleep in death, but their condition is spoken of as "resting" and "being comforted." But at the second coming of Jesus, when the saints rise in the first resurrection, there are scores of Scripture passages that describe the powers, the activities and ministries of the glorified saints, as coming back from the wedding supper with Jesus (Rev. 19:11, 14), and as taking part with Christ in judging the world, and the wicked nations (Psa. 149:5-9), and as sitting with Christ on His millennial throne (Luke 22: 28-30 and Rev. 2:26, 27), and as exercising authority as princes and priests over all nations during the thousand-year reign of Christ (Rev. 20:4-6 and Dan. 7:27); all of which opens up to us the peculiar joys of heavenly royalty. There is a joy in the handling of great wealth, and in the exercise of authority and power, which, when it shall be absolutely free from all self-seeking, from all foolishness or severity or indiscretion, and exercised in boundless love and wisdom, will be indeed a royal joy and a drop from that infinite happiness that God has in the exercise of His absolute dominion over all His creation. The saints will enjoy their rewards, and as the songs of the reapers in the harvest field attest their gladness in gathering the golden grain, so at the end of this age, when the harvest of the precious blood is reaped, and the rewards are given to God's faithful ones, they will not be empty honors, but various kinds of substantial happiness. And beyond the millennium, the glorified saints will have an immense service of ministry to many worlds and generations in the ever-increasing kingdom of God; for we are told in the Greek that God will show forth "His glory in the church, by Christ Jesus, throughout all the generations of the age of the ages." Eph. 3:21.

6. *The Joy of the Beatific Vision.* To see God's face in cloudless light, to gaze in rapturous adoration upon the unimaginable beauties of the countenance of the Almighty, will be the crown, the uttermost limit, of all the joys of heaven. All the pleasures of our glorified senses, and the delights of our illuminated intellects, and the expansion of our faculties in the resurrected state, and the sweet meltings of celestial love, and the gladness of heavenly society, and of our multiplied ministries, are but twilight joys, are but the outer fringes of heavenly bliss, compared with that ecstatic awe, that ineffable gladness of seeing the face of God. We shall see the glory of the three divine Persons beaming from the face of our blessed Lord Jesus. And then, through the avenue of His glorified humanity, our spiritual eyes will gaze undazzled on the three personalities in the blazing fires of the Godhead, each distinctly recognized and adored and loved, with such heavenly passion of joy as would burst the vessels of our created natures, unless they were girded with glorified capacities. We shall see the eternal generation of the Son in the bosom of the Father, and we shall watch the ever-radiant procession of the Holy Ghost from the Father and the Son, like a gulf stream of whitest fire, ever streaming forth as it did before the worlds were made, as it flows now and

will continue to pour forth in an endless flow of the mutual love of the Father and the Son to endless ages. We shall see the unity of the Divine essence, and the simplicity of the Divine nature, and all the beautiful attributes of the Divine character, shining in their unchanging beauty through all the changes of creation's history. We shall know the meaning and the full fruition of those crowning words, "Come, ye blessed of my Father, inherit the kingdom prepared for you from the foundation of the world," "enter thou into the joy of thy Lord." To feel God sensibly near us, and His spiritual presence in us, is the greatest joy of earth; so to see Him face to face will be the crowning joy of heaven.

> "When the last feeble step has been taken
>   And the gates of that city appear,
> And the beautiful songs of the angels
>   Float out on my listening ear;
> When all that now seems so mysterious
>   Will be bright and as clear as the day,
> Then the toils of the road will seem nothing,
>   When I get to the end of the way."

PREACH THE LORD'S COMING.

By E. P. Marvin.

"There has been much error and fanaticism connected with it." Yes, and with every other Bible doctrine. "Prove all things; hold fast that which is good." Most of the heresies of to-day come from the unsanctified learning of Post-millennialists, and most of the worldliness of the churches comes from those who say: "My Lord delayeth His coming."

"Well, we know all men must die, and death is the Lord's coming to me."

Two mistakes. It is declared in the New Testament that we shall not all die, but a generation of saints will go like Enoch and Elijah, and no two events stand in stronger contrast than death and our Lord's coming.

"But if I am a Christian shall I not be saved and all right?" You will be saved, but not all right, for your crown of reward, unless you obey the plain and repeated command to watch.

"The prophecies are mysterious, and I really do not get time to study this subject of the Lord's coming."

About one-third of this whole Bible is prophecy. Will you neglect or slight this third of God's revelation?

Take time, dear brother, from something else of less

importance and study this subject, now rising into such towering prominence. Stop trying to run the world and all sorts of societies and clubs in the church.

The Jews were reproved again and again for not studying and understanding their own prophecies. Indeed, it was on account of this neglect and blindness that they rejected and crucified the Lord.

A special benediction is pronounced on him that readeth and heareth the great prophetic book of the New Testament. Rev. 1:3. Perhaps if we should put this doctrine into the form of a popular novel and infuse it with heresy, some of our preachers would find time to read it and give it a pulpit boom.

"But it paralyzes missions and cuts the nerve of Christian endeavor."

How can truth paralyze the cause of truth? The proud fiction of taking the world for Christ cannot do as much good as the truth. But the most practical answer to this objection to preaching the Lord's coming can be found in lives, such as those of Spurgeon, Guinness, Muller, Hudson Taylor, and nearly all the evangelists in the world, as well as most of those now going to foreign missions.

"I do not want to make a hobby of it." Very well, but how many times have you preached upon it? "I do not know as I have ever done it at all." Then do not fear as yet.

"Well, it makes the gospel a failure and Christianity a defeated power."

If the gospel had promised the conversion of the world in this dispensation, or even any one nation of the world, it would have been a most dismal failure for the last eighteen hundred years.

It promised an election of grace, a Gentile Bride called out of the nations for the Son of God.

It has succeeded in the purpose for which it was sent. Acts 15:14-17; Luke 19:13.

Post-millennarians make the gospel a failure.

Never has any country, city or hamlet been "taken for Christ."

All who labor faithfully to fulfill the Great Commission will attain a triumphant success and a glorious reward.

It is not true among sinners that "all truth has power to authenticate itself." Men do not take the remedy and on this account are lost.

Christ and the Apostles never staked the truth of Christianity on its prevalence. Mohammedanism has made far more rapid progress than Christianity, and Buddhism has far more adherents. A religion may spread, either because of its truth that appeals to the higher nature of man, or because of its error that appeals to his baser nature.

Success is doing your duty. Faithfulness brings the reward. Matt. 25:21.

Let me kindly and earnestly entreat my brethren in the gospel ministry to candidly and prayerfully consider the following reasons for preaching the Coming of the Lord:

1. Christ and the Apostles command us to preach the whole truth, and especially this part of revelation. Acts. 20:26-27; Tit. 2:15; Rev. 22:10.

2. Christ and the Apostles preached it almost constantly, speaking of it in the New Testament more than 300 times. The Apostles preached, not "Jesus and death," but "Jesus and the resurrection."

Almost every page presents examples.

The Old Testament speaks of the Second Coming more than ten times as often as of the First Coming. The Apostolic Church held and taught the imminence of the Lord's coming and watched for it. 1 Cor. 1:7; 1 Thess. 1:9-10. They would have doubted the piety of one who did not love his appearing. 2 Tim. 4:8.

3. We sin at a dear rate if for sinister motives we neglect to study and preach this doctrine. Never before was so much clear light thrown upon it, and never before were we so near this grand event. It requires strong willfulness to shut the eyes to this flood of light now overflowing Christendom. Luke 12:47; John 12:35; Rev. 22:18-19.

Wonderful progress is being made in these last times in the study and interpretation of prophecy.

4. We may well fear a blight on our ministry for this neglect, and we shall certainly suffer loss when the Lord comes, if we are unfaithful heralds of His coming. It is already manifest that the evangelists and ministers who love and preach "that blessed hope" are most blest in winning souls and edifying the body of Christ. They preach a full, rich gospel. The most heavenly man of the Old Testament is Daniel, and of the New Testament the Prophet John, the special prophets of the Lord's Second Coming. Study prayerfully Matt. 7:22-27; 24:48-51; Heb. 9:28; 10:25-37.

May God save us from the fate of those who do not "look for Him," nor "love His Appearing." Who can tell what it will be?

5. This is "present truth" of ever-increasing moment and fitting adaptation to the times, as "we see the day approaching."

Some truths are always equally important, while others have a special, temporary or local importance. The ministry of Enoch, Noah, Jonah, Lot and John the Baptist pertains to the latter class. As God heralded judgments and warned men through them, so in these "last times" no small part of our ministry should herald,

> "The King that comes in mercy;
>   The King that comes in might;
> To terminate the evil
>   And diadem the right."

Matt. 24:45-46; 16:3; 25:6. The Holy Spirit shows us things to come. John 14:26.

6. Preaching the imminence of the Lord's coming is a vehicle of reviving power for the Laodicean church, and of salvation for sinners. Enoch used it with the Ante-diluvian apostates. Jude, 14:15.

If the professing church had been blessed with a faithful ministry and leadership in the teaching and preaching of this "Blessed Hope," it would not have been in its present unbelief and worldliness.

This is emphatically a separating and a purifying hope. It Separates, Consecrates and Concentrates its devotees. I do not know a church in which this blessed hope is faithfully preached and vitally believed that has dancers, card players or theater goers in it, or that would hold a fair, festival or entertainment to raise money.

If anything can arouse the Bride from her slumbers, her frivolity, or from dallying in the lap of the Christ-rejecting world, it must be the advent cries of the coming Bridegroom, Judge and King, scattered all through the New Testament, and surely nothing can arouse the sinner like the solemn proclamation of that day of wrath which will come as a snare, like a thief, like a flash of lightning! "Maranatha" should be our watchword in these last times.

7. This proclamation is a prophetic means of hastening the coming, the crowning and the kingdom. It helps to bring in the Gentile Bride, by stimulating to the fulfillment of the great commission. Matt. 24:14; 2 Pet. 3:12.

Directly contrary to the theory of some who oppose us, or at least fear evil from our doctrine, the preaching of it by pastors, evangelists and missionaries has been used of God as the chief means of reviving the missionary spirit of the present generation. Its rare and reviving power is filling the world with devoted missionaries and loving evangelists. Study it and preach it, my brother.

KADESH—BARNEA.

REV. EVAN H. HOPKINS.

Where and What was Kadesh-Barnea?

Text, Deut. 1 :19.

In the second verse of this chapter, in a parenthesis, we are told that it was a place eleven days' journey from Horeb. But that does not greatly help us. What was Kadesh-Barnea? Where was it? What were its characteristics? Kadesh-Barnea lay upon the southern frontier of Canaan, just where the rolling downs of Southern Canaan descended into the desert sand, just there upon the frontier, on the borderland between Canaan and the terrible wilderness.

Israel had spent a whole year at Horeb. There the undisciplined rabble had become a marshalled army; there they had put away many of the customs and habits which had clung to them from long association with the Egyptians, and as God's sacramental host they had passed out of the wonderful natural temple constituted by the mountains of Sinai, and across the desert waste. Ah, how glad their hearts were—what a quiver of joy passed through the host from the foremost to the rearmost ranks, as they cried, "We are reaching the land;

we are coming near to the hills of Canaan;" and when they could descry in the dim blue mist the outlines at last of the rolling country which they knew was covered with vineyards, olive-yards, and pasture-lands!

It must have been as grateful to these weary people, who had spent these months in gazing only upon ragged crags and traversing the sand dunes, to see those outlines of the hills of Canaan, as it was afterwards to the crew of Columbus to turn their gaze from the weary waste of waters to descry the outlines of the fair country that he sought. Oh, the joy of it! Oh, the triumph of it, to feel that the desert was behind, that Canaan was really in front, that a few more days must pass, and only a few, before they stood within their inheritance, the land which God had bound Himself to give to their fathers. Oh, blessed, blessed vision! Up came Moses, the law-giver, the princes of Israel, the warriors, the priests, the Levites with their sacred burden, the women with the children—they all came at last up from the desert, and felt beneath their feet the soft sward of Palestine that seemed to announce that at last their long, weary journey was at an end.

They did not realize that they were to retreat from that point, and go back again into the wilderness from which they were emerging. It never entered their minds to suppose that forty years of wandering were to intervene between that moment and the other moment when they should cross the Jordan to inherit the land. They little deemed that one by one all that host, which seemed like the flowers upon the meadows of May, was to fall before the reaper's scythe of death; that two only were to enter the land; and that their children, who were growing up around them, young men and women under the age of twenty, were to take their own place before God's promise was fulfilled.

All this, of course, is intended to supply some deep lesson for ourselves. Probably there is not one person who is truly converted to God that has not at some time come to Kadesh-Barnea. Some have come thither and passed that way into the land of promise. Some have come thither and settled down, and remain always between the desert on the one hand and the land of rest on the other, sometimes making an incursion into the one and then an incursion into the other, but living a border life between them. Perhaps some years ago you came to Kadesh-barnea, but were bidden to retreat from it. Perhaps you look back upon one radiant moment when you were nearer God, nearer rest, nearer peace, nearer the fruition of the perfect life than you have ever been since. Since that moment you have been treading again the desert waste, and have known the infinite bitterness of its restlessness, its weariness, its hunger and thirst. Every soul in the course of its pilgrimage comes presently to Kadesh-barnea.

Let us be very precise that we make no mistake. *Kadesh-barnea does not stand for regeneration.* Regeneration may be set forth in the fact that Israel in Egypt was God's child, though bound beneath the bondage of Pharaoh and groaning beneath the tale of bricks, often lashed by the scourge—the cruel knout. Therefore, whatever Kadesh-barnea stands for, it does not represent the fact of the new birth by the Word and

Spirit of God. You must be born again before you can
come to Kadesh-barnea; but you may have been born
again and yet never have come out of Egypt; or you
may have come out of Egypt and reached Sinai and
never come to Kadesh-barnea. It is not enough for you
to say that you are God's children; there are heights beyond depths of experience, much more to know and experience.

*Kadesh-barnea does not stand for redemption by
blood.* This is set forth by the Paschal Lamb, the
sprinkled blood, the exodus in that night which was
much to be remembered. The people needed to be redeemed before they could come to Kadesh-barnea,but being redeemed did not necessarily involve the attainment
of Kadesh-barnea. Is it not so with you? You may
have been born from above; may know what it is to
have been redeemed by the blood of Jesus, and yet there
is something beyond in your experience. You have never come to Kadesh-barnea.

I. What, then, Does Kadesh-barnea Stand for?

It stands for that moment in a man's life when he
has the opportunity of forsaking the wilderness and entering into the land of rest. And what does the wilderness stand for?

(1) *Kadesh is rest.* The wilderness stands for purposeless wandering. If you were to trace, with the help
of the Book of Numbers, which enumerates the successive encampments of Israel, the course of the people
through the wilderness, you would find it was zigzag,
backwards and forwards, again and again going over
the same ground, making no regular advance towards

their goal. So it is in much of our life. There is too
much purposeless wandering. We start up to do a deed
for God, but presently fail in it, relinquish our activity,
and drop back into inertia. We say to ourselves: We
will be pure, and strong, and holy; but after awhile the
wing flags, the speed stays, and we, who have burned for
a moment like seraphs, search vainly our hearts to find
one spark of light and heat. How much of our life has
been filled with these zigzag and unsatisfactory experiences, tracing and retracing, always learning the same
lessons, sitting on the same form, put back to the old
experiences, but never coming to the knowledge of the
truth!

Kadesh-barnea, on the other hand, stands for the
moment in a man's life when he for evermore quits and
leaves this wretched, unsatisfactory experience, and with
a purpose in his heart, cries: "Leaving the things that
are behind, I press towards the goal for the prize of my
high calling of God in Christ Jesus."

(2) *Kadesh stands for satisfaction.* The wilderness stands for want, for unsatisfied longing. God suffered them to hunger and thirst. It seems as though
they were never content. Whatever God did for them
or did not do, they murmured at it. However lavishly
He spread their table, they longed for the leeks and
garlicks and onions of the Nile. Why did He not let
us die in the wilderness? Why did He not allow us to
find our graves in Egypt? Why has He brought us here
to die of thirst and hunger? Oh, the constant dissatisfaction of the wilderness life. This has had its coun-
terpart with each of us, always thirsting for satisfac-

tion; but, as in the fable of Tantalus, the water always
evading the thirsty lips which are put down to slake
their burning fever; always going to the well to draw,
and bringing the water back in a leaking pitcher, which
as we reach home is found to be empty; always gathering
the apples which turn out to be rotten;—the apples of
Sodom. Oh, how often we have thought, if God were
to give me this, all my days would be filled with music,
with the light and warmth of summer! but when God
has given our heart's desire, leanness has come into our
soul.

But Kadesh-barnea is the moment in a man's life
when he leaves behind the dissatisfaction, the desires
which are never perfectly at rest, when he discovers the
truth of what Jesus said: "He that drinketh of the
water that I shall give him shall never thirst, but it
shall be in him a spring of water rising up into everlasting life."

(3) *Kadesh stands for Victory.* The wilderness
stands for failure and defeat. The enemies sweep
around the camp and cut off the stragglers; Israel is not
able to hold its own against Amalek, or if it does for a
brief interval, then Amalek, which stands for the flesh,
presently gathers to itself new force and overcomes. The
wilderness is always the land of defeat. You prize yourself that you are going to conquer this time—you even
pray that you may; you vow that you will; you wonder
that you have ever yielded before; you argue with yourself against ever yielding again; you say to yourself: "I
shall not yield this time, I will be strong; why can I
not be man enough to put my foot upon the neck of this

evil thing? Why should I not be a conqueror?" You
go into the battle full of self-confidence; but before ever
the battle has waxed hot you find yourself trampled in
the very dust of defeat; your brave weapons are broken
around you, your armor hacked through and splintered
to pieces. But Kadesh-barnea is the point in a man's
life when he leaves behind this weary experience of defeat, and enters into that life of victory where no evil
thing is able to stand against him, and he goes from
victory to victory through Him that loved him.

Where are you today? Are you still in the wilderness
of purposeless wandering; still hungering and thirsting; still vanquished and overcome? O, poor soul, why
should you not this very day come up to Kadesh-barnea,
not merely to touch it and see the land beyond, not to so-
journ in its homes for one brief hour, but to live there,
and to make it the starting-point from which you should
go forward into ever new experience of the rest, satisfaction, and victory which accrue from faith? That,
then, is what Kadesh-barnea stands for. Have you
passed it, or are you living in it, or have you not come
to it as yet?

II. WHAT MADE THE DIFFERENCE IN THE EXPERI-
ENCE OF THE PEOPLE THAT VISITED KADESH-BARNEA?

The answer is certain—*Unbelief*, which showed itself in many ways. First, it manifested itself by send-
ing the spies to examine the land. Surely that was a
great mistake. When God gives aught to us, we should
receive it without inquiring as to its worth and value.
The fact that God had promised to give this land, and
that He had pledged His troth that it flowed with milk

and honey, was surely enough to silence every question.
How came it that they *spied* out the land? Was not
that very impertinent act of theirs a confession that
they did not perfectly trust the Word of God?

The second manifestation of the spirit of unbelief
was that, through the eyes of the ten spies, they considered its cities and the giants to the exclusion of God.
There were giants certainly, and cities walled up to heav-
en; there were immense difficulties confronting them,
which might be viewed in different ways. The ten, who
followed the devices of their own hearts, spelled giants
with a capital *G*, and God with a little *g*. But the two,
though they saw these difficulties, had such a view of
God's omnipotence that they spelt giant with a little *g*,
and God with a capital. God filled their horizon; God
seemed all-sufficient for their need; and they said, If
He delight in us, He is well able to bring us in and give
us the land. It was the difference between unbelief
and faith, between looking at circumstances first and
God second, or looking at God first and circumstances
afterwards; the difference that comes to all of us is as to
whether we are going to magnify the difficulty or magnify the name of Jehovah, who does wonderful things for
those who trust Him.

Have you learned this elementary lesson? It seems
impossible that you should ever move with a direct intention towards the goal of your life; that you will ever
be satisfied in this world; that you should ever cease
from being overcome by your enemies or have the victory; but if you will learn the lesson of today, and no
longer count on your poor resources, but live looking

for everything from God, then you will have
rest and victory. The moment your soul hangs
on God and expects everything from Him, you leave the
Kadesh-barnea behind forever, and enter into the land
of rest where God is the one all-sufficient answer to every
doubt and fear, every misgiving and dread.

III. How Are We To Obtain this Faith that
Carries Us Beyond the Frontier into the Land of
Rest?

In the Epistle to the Hebrews (ch. iv.), we have it
stated exactly: *Cease from your own works.* "He that is
entered into his own rest, he also hath ceased from his
own works, as God did from His." It is your own fussy
activity which is invalidating everything. You remember how, in the old mythologic fable, the goddess took
her child and dipped him in the immortalizing river,
and he was made impervious to any weapon, except at
the heel by which she held him; it was there he was shot
with the fatal arrow. If you trust in God ninety-nine
parts of a hundred, but in the hundredth part are relying
on your own works, prayers, preparation or tears, you
may depend upon it that that will invalidate everything.
We get rest only when, by the grace of God, we cease
from our own works that we may enter into His; and,
having made Him first, begin to work, not up to His
help, but down from it. Cease from your own works
that you may work the works of God. Cease from your
own energy that the energy of God may operate
through you. Cease from self, that God may be all in
all, and originate more abiding results than you could
ever have achieved.

Cease from your sinful works. If there is any known sin in your life which you cherish, which you cuddle and fondle in your bosom, which you feel you want and will not renounce, remember, as long as it is not judged, it will invalidate your faith. You cannot trust God absolutely whilst you make provision for the flesh to fulfil the lust thereof. You must, in the intention of your will and the choice of your heart, cease from sinful works.

Cease from legal works. Too often we have sought to justify ourselves before God; to do things which would make ourselves more pleasing in His sight; we have forgotten that our righteousnesses were as filthy rags. We, like Cain, have brought the fruits of our own producing. But we must put away our legal works, our own righteousness, our own efforts to sanctify ourselves. We are not saved by works, but created in Christ for them.

Cease from selfish works. We must endeavor to be good, earnest, and obedient, not because of any profit that may accrue, but for God's sake and because it is right.

Cease from your sinful works: from your legal works; from works that have self as the pivot and centre. Have done with it all, and taking up the foot which has so long touched the shelving bottom of the beach, launch yourself upon the upbearing wave. You will never know what the buoyant water will do until you have trusted it. Let yourself go, and then, when God is all and in all, when you let God do in and through you the purpose of His will, then the wilderness life of the seventh of Romans is abandoned for the Canaan life of the eighth chapter; then you leave Kadesh-barnea for the Land of Promise.

But if you refuse, there is nothing for it but for you to turn back and go for your forty years of wandering. A child?—Yes. Redeemed?—Yes. Destined to go to heaven? Yes. But missing, fatally missing, that blessedness which in this life is within the reach of those who through faith and patience inherit the promises—Consecrated Life.

BIBLE FRUIT.

OR, A SERIES OF BIBLE READINGS.

TWO HUNDRED MAPS

L. L. PICKETT ONE DOLLAR.

You perhaps never saw a book on the future of this earth. This book will meet this want.

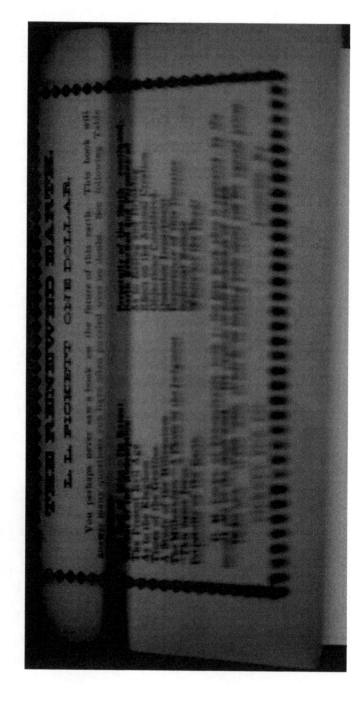

BIBLE FRUIT,

BEING A SERIES OF BIBLE READINGS,

By L. L. PICKETT,

ASSISTED IN THE SELECTIONS BY

Rev. W. N. MATHENEY,

To which are Chapters Contributed by Several

Different Writers.

CLOTH, $1.00.   PAPER, 50c.

1899.

PICKETT PUBLISHING CO.,
LOUISVILLE, KY.

BRANCH ⟨ Greenville, Texas.

THE RENEWED EARTH.

L. L. PICKETT ONE DOLLAR,

You perhaps never saw a book on the future of this earth. This book will answer many questions you have often puzzled over no doubt. See following Table of Contents:

The Fall of Man—Its Extent.
Extent of the Redemption.
The Present Evil Age.
As to the Kingdom.
Times of the Gentiles.
A Study of the Millennium.
The Millennium—A Phase of the Judgment.
"This Same Jesus."
Perpetuity of the Earth.

Perpetuity of the Earth—continued.
Earth Renewed and Perpetuated.
As to Eating and Drinking.
Effect on the Animal Creation.
Objections Considered.
Question Department.
Importance of this Doctrine.
Spiritual Results.
Where are the Dead?

D. M. Locke, of Pennsylvania, took 12 the first week after it appeared, 25 the second and 70 the third week   He expects to sell hundreds of copies. Order now. If you wish to sell it, in making your order ask for agents' prices.

PICKETT PUB. CO.,   -   -   -   -   Louisville, Ky.

PROVERBS.

"A New Book of Proverbs; or the Economy of Human Life."

Yes, Proverbs.

This is the title of a new book recently arranged
for the press by Evangelist Luther R. Robinson.
It is an entirely different book from anything now
before the American people so far as is known,
It is

AN ANCIENT SYSTEM OF MORALITY

containing hundreds of proverbs of marvelous pro-
duction, in some respects similar to the Proverbs
of Solomon, yet treating many more different
subjects.

Every age, stage and condition in life, from the
cradle to the grave, is treated in

A MASTERLY AND PROVERBIAL

way. This book will hold spell-bound all alike,
old and young, rich and poor, learned or unlearned.

Secure a copy and read till you laugh, shout and cry,

A Fine Book For Your Children.

CLOTH, 50c.   PAPER, 25c.

PICKETT PUB. CO., LOUISVILLE, KY.

Lightning Source UK Ltd.
Milton Keynes UK
UKHW020637050323
418046UK00007B/792